CW00373511

THEIR OWN ACCOUNTS:
VIEWS OF PROMINENT 20th CENTURY
ACCOUNTANTS

by

Michael Mumford

Published by

The Institute of Chartered Accountants of Scotland
CA House, 21 Haymarket Yards
Edinburgh EH12 5BH

First Published 2007
The Institute of Chartered Accountants of Scotland

© 2007
ISBN 978-1-904574-36-1
EAN 9781904574361

This book is published for the Research Committee of
The Institute of Chartered Accountants of Scotland.
The views expressed in this report are those of the author and the
interviewees and do not necessarily represent the views of
the Council of the Institute or the Research Committee.

No responsibility for loss occasioned to any person acting
or refraining from action as a result of any material
in this publication can be accepted by the author or publisher.

All rights reserved. No part of this publication may be
reproduced, stored in a retrieval system, or transmitted, in
any form or by any means, electronic, mechanical, photocopy,
recording or otherwise, without prior permission of the publisher.

Printed and bound in Great Britain
by T. J. International Ltd.

C ONTENTS

FOREWORD

This research report was funded to enable the transcription of interviews with prominent accountants that Michael Mumford had carried out in the late 1970s/early 1980s, but had not completed at that time for reasons he explains in this report. It is clear from reading the interviews that issues which are highly relevant today were also of concern in the mid-twentieth century, such as the use of judgement and the level of detail required in accounting standards. The interviews provide a valuable insight into the development of the profession and accounting practice, and an understanding of where we are today.

The current day relevance of many issues discussed in the interviews is illustrated by Jack Clayton's ahead of time views on the risk of final salary pension schemes. He opposed such schemes on the grounds that no director of a company has the right to issue post dated cheques of an unknown amount – least of all a government minister. This issue continues to be high on the political and business agenda as final salary schemes continue to have funding problems. Another issue which has come to the fore in recent years, and a campaign issue for ICAS, is the need for principles rather than rules in accounting standards. This is clearly illustrated in the interview with Bruce Sutherland where he discusses the need for a basic concept of conveying information in a meaningful form to a reasonably informed reader of accounts.

Twelve of the nearly thirty interviews carried out by Michael Mumford have been transcribed. Four of these are included within the published report; transcripts of the remaining eight interviews are available on the ICAS website www.icas.org.uk/research. The interviews cover the twentieth century, which was a period of significant change, with the advent of the Second World War, the influence of US accounting practices, the growth of large-scale companies, the divorce of ownership and control, and a growing securities market. New accounting problems emerged and key issues noted from the interviews included: recognition of income; taxation; accounting for changing prices; group accounting; accounting standards; and management costing.

The transcription of the interviews and this publication has been funded by the Scottish Accountancy Trust for Education and Research (SATER). The Research Committee of ICAS has also been happy to support this publication. The Committee recognises that the views expressed do not necessarily represent those of ICAS itself, but hopes that the recollections of the interviewees provide an insight into how the profession has developed and a historical context for relevant current day accounting issues.

David Spence
Convener
Research Committee
November 2007

ACKNOWLEDGEMENTS

My first debt is to those people who agreed to be interviewed and who gave me generously of their time and experience. Twelve interviews are included in this study, but there were another fifteen or so that have not been transcribed here. In chronological order, the twelve interviews were with E. Kenneth Wright, Lawrence W. Robson, Dr. Stanley Dixon, Eric Hay Davison, Jack Clayton, Dr. Norman G. Lancaster, Sir Basil Smallpeice, William W. Fea, Bruce Sutherland, Professor W.T. Baxter, Harry Norris and Godfrey Judd. I am grateful to them all. I was delighted to be able to discuss their transcriptions by letter and telephone with Bruce Sutherland, Will Baxter, Harry Norris and Godfrey Judd, although I am sad to say that Professor Baxter died soon afterwards.

I am grateful also to five sons and one daughter of those interviewed, who read and commented on draft transcriptions where the person involved had died during the period of almost thirty years since the interviews took place. These include Liz Aitken and David Wright; Roger Dixon; Ian Hay Davison; Jeremy Lancaster; and Mr. J.M.W. Fea. It is with regret that I was not able to trace relatives of Jack Clayton or Sir Basil Smallpeice despite a careful search and the help of the editor of the journal Accountancy.

As noted in the Introduction to the study, my original interviews were funded by the late Professor Edward Stamp and the International Centre for Research in Accounting at the University of Lancaster. I am very grateful for the encouragement of Professor Stephen Zeff, Herbert S. Autrey Professor of Accounting, Jesse H. Jones Graduate School of Management, Rice University, Texas, who urged publication of the study.

The task of converting the interview tapes into book form was made possible by the skill and application of Cheryl Scott (who transcribed the tapes), and of members of staff of the Institute of Chartered Accountants of Scotland (ICAS) – in particular, Isobel Webber and Richard Anderson, and latterly Angie Wilkie and Michelle Crickett (Assistant Director, Accounting and Auditing). I am also grateful to members of the ICAS Research Committee, to the referees (whose suggestions improved the book significantly), and to those who produced the printed book and the electronic interview records available on the website.

I present the interview records with few embellishments or added notes. It would have substantially lengthened the text if footnotes had been used to explain contemporary references and correct occasional misstatements. It was not my aim to provide a factually corrected record of interviews that were extempore and without notes. Subject to this, the faults that remain are my responsibility.

Finally, the Research Committee and the researchers are grateful for the financial support of the Trustees of the Scottish Accountancy Trust for Education and Research without which the publication would not have been possible.

INTRODUCTION

'Times are changing and accounting conventions will change with them. Today, study of the historical development of accounting conventions and of the causes which have brought about change may be more useful than a description of present practice.'

George O. May (1943, p9)

Preliminary comments

In the late 1970s, whilst I was head of the Department of Accounting and Finance at Lancaster University, one of the major international accountancy firms came to recruit students. I was invited to dinner with the team, headed by a Lancaster graduate in languages, who was partner in charge of a regional office. Over dinner, he and I discussed some new requirements for nationalised industries to report replacement costs. After a while, the youngest member of the group commented that she was a graduate in languages who had qualified as a chartered accountant three or four years earlier, and this was the first time she had ever heard a discussion of accounting theory. At this point, the two other men present said they were both science graduates, qualified for five or six years - and neither of them, either, had previously heard a discussion of accounting theory. I found it sad and rather shocking that three very bright accountants, in one of the top firms, knew accounting only as a purely technical activity. They seemingly lacked any theoretical basis or understanding of its social and economic consequences.

Thirty years later the situation has not much improved. Indeed, in some respects matters have got worse. The need to memorise the details of complex accounting standards increasingly distances accounting trainees from a conceptual grasp of what financial reports are supposed to mean or accomplish. The UK Accounting Standards Board today operates with a form of conceptual statement that would have been unrecognisable at the time of the interviews. It also typifies the accounting profession, particularly in the United Kingdom, as being 'unlearned' to an extent that practitioners of law or medicine, for example, would simply not comprehend.

Furthermore, accountants lack a sense of the historical context in which they work. They rarely ask where accountancy rules originated, or how, or why. Their trainers discourage this in any case in the context of professional exams. What matters to them is the pass rate!

It is the function of this monograph not to defend accountancy, but to record some of its history. The book records interviews with four men who were senior and highly regarded in the profession. Eight more interviews, also all with men, are being published at the same time, in electronic form, accessible over the internet from the Institute of Chartered Accountants of Scotland - www.icas.org.uk/research

At many points, the twelve men discuss theoretical issues, often with insight and conviction - yet their views often differ from one another. It would not be easy to predict the points on which they would all have agreed in discussion around a table. The interviews are instructive about the way that the profession - in particular, the Institute of Chartered Accountants in England and Wales (ICAEW), to which 11 of the 12 men belonged - came to develop in the middle decades of the 20th century.

Moreover, despite the fact that the interviews were conducted nearly thirty years ago, many of the observations are still relevant today. For example, Kenneth Wright talks about the meticulous planning that preceded the merger in 1957 between the ICAEW and the Society of

Incorporated Accountants and Auditors (SIAA) - the last successful merger between accountancy bodies in the UK - at a time when he chaired the London Society of Chartered Accountants. There have been several notable, and costly, failures since then to merge, five involving the ICAEW, the latest in 2005 (see *Accountancy*, October and November 2005). Shackleton and Walker (1998 and 2001) present comprehensive analyses of the unsuccessful mergers attempts between 1957 and 1970, showing the difficult issues involved, particularly in multi-party mergers. The merger of the SIAA with the three chartered institutes (of Scotland, in England and Wales, and in Ireland) was, by contrast, somewhat more straightforward. Nevertheless, the later attempts all overlooked the lessons of 1957: the small margin that often decides such votes; the detailed planning and insight required beforehand; the diplomacy involved; and the need for an acute sense of history.

My programme of interviews was set up in 1978, when I began to contact and talk to some eminent members of the profession to ask them about their experiences. My late friend and colleague, Eddie Stamp, through the International Centre for Research in Accounting at Lancaster University Management School, paid for the costs and I recorded the interviews with a tape recorder. Getting tapes transcribed in the 1980s proved a nightmare. The typewritten pages usually needed to be re-typed more than once to achieve a readable version, and this was taking many, many hours. I, therefore, put the project away, uncompleted.

In December 2001, as we walked around Tarn Howes in the English Lake District, I told Professor Steve Zeff about the interviews, and he encouraged me to resume the task and to approach The Institute of Chartered Accountants of Scotland, which has a reputation for supporting and publishing historical research (for example, Walker, 2005), for a grant to pay for the transcription of these interviews from thirty years ago. I then selected twelve of the interviews to edit for publication. Cheryl Scott soon had the drafts word-processed on disk, and I set about editing the spoken words into readable form, removing some duplication and, very occasionally, passages 'off the record', and in places improving grammar or syntax that would not be noticed in speech but would jar in print.

I decided not to insert footnotes in the interviews (for example, to explain technical references that arose to UK Statements of Standards Accounting Practice (SSAPs) currently in force). Some of the things said in the interviews are, quite frankly, wrong, and I gave a lot of thought as to whether I should point these out in footnotes. I decided against, for two reasons: I could not take on the role of vouching every statement, and, moreover, putting in footnotes would severely break up the flow of the dialogue. However, I use brackets in the interview records to add some selected comments where I think they may help the reader. Many of the facts are in any case quite easy to check independently, such as the dates of legal cases and the full citation of SSAPs.

The interviews are published now in the belief that they give some picture of the profession in the mid-20th century - albeit, a rather partial view, from the perspective of an unusually successful small group of people, most of whom knew the others as members of the ICAEW Council and most of whom had served on district societies first.

Obtaining permission to publish the texts, thirty years after the recordings were made, was a challenge, but I was able to meet the ethical guidelines of the Oral History Society. I was glad to be able to talk on the telephone to four of the people interviewed, and they read and commented in writing on the transcriptions. Sadly, one of them, Will Baxter, has since died. In six other cases, sons or daughters read and approved the drafts. I am very grateful to all the people who gave their approval to the interview texts. In two cases - Basil Smallpeice and Jack Clayton - unfortunately I could not trace any family members.

Before commenting on the people interviewed individually, I will briefly set out the broad historical context of their work and explain some of the technical problems in accounting that gave difficulties to them and their colleagues.

A historical context: accounting for large-scale enterprises

The 1844 Joint Stock Companies Act in Britain was not the earliest company legislation, but it was particularly important because it enabled companies to be formed, by a simple process of registration, more cheaply and easily than before, and registered company numbers rose rapidly. Another act, in 1855, permitted companies to be registered with limited liability, to protect the members from being personally liable for the debts of the company, although this increased the risks for the creditors. Companies were obliged to keep accounts and report to members yearly on a balance sheet that had been checked by auditors drawn from amongst them, to be put on record at the Companies Registry.

It was, however, the growth of companies in America, after the end of the Civil War in 1865, which led to unprecedented demands for capital, and also to the greatest new challenges in accounting. The capital for all this investment came largely from Europe, from investors who could neither observe nor dominate the managers who had day-to-day control of their resources. Share capital came to be divided amongst large numbers of individual investors, living far away and relying on poor communications, with little chance of getting together to exert effective control over the directors. The investment risks were great, but the prospective returns were so high that the risks were worth taking.

Thus developed the 'divorce between ownership and control', analysed in detail by Berle and Means (1932, revised edition 1968) which later became the context for the analysis of 'agency theory'. In fact, by 1968, in Britain and well as in the USA, share ownership was already coming to be concentrated in fewer hands as institutional investors (pensions and insurance funds, in particular) acquired legal ownership of shares on behalf of the policy-holders whom they represented. The institutions remained reluctant, however, to exploit their market power over the corporations they were increasingly coming to own. These people were portfolio managers, not captains of industry - they were not able to tell the directors of a steel mill how to produce steel, or retail stores how to run their businesses.

The modern, large-scale, managerially controlled corporation, described by Chandler (1977 and 1990), tended to still be an American phenomenon at that time. Back in Great Britain, large-scale businesses were also growing in the 19th century, but on a smaller scale and often with simpler organisational structures. Companies in Britain, as in the rest of Europe, were still typically run by the proprietor's family, whereas American companies were increasingly managed by professional salaried managers, often trained in post-graduate university business schools, a trend that exacerbated the problem described by agency theory. American managers were very effective in growing and innovating the businesses they controlled, devising new techniques of strategy, mass production, marketing and standard costing that were not brought to Britain until the 1930s. It is no surprise that Basil Smallpeice sought to join an American company as soon as he moved into industry, or that Bruce Sutherland, Will Baxter, Godfrey Judd and Lawrence Robson all went there for extended visits early in their careers.

Within mainland Europe, with nearly all companies still controlled by proprietors and their family members, any need for additional external capital was usually met by banks, which took partial ownership of share capital as a means of participating in the direction and rewards of the business. In Britain, by contrast, the banks altered their investment patterns drastically after the collapse of the City of Glasgow Bank in 1878. British bankers took to lending money, mainly on short term overdrafts, rather than getting involved in holding shares, which implied a responsibility for running the companies in which they were invested. After 1880, in the UK as in the US, companies started to raise new external capital from the stock exchanges, rather than from banks. Financial reporting took on greater significance in the context of these growing securities markets.

As noted above, difficult new problems arose in accounting for these new large enterprises. The long-established techniques of double-entry bookkeeping had to be adapted to deal with them, and controversies often arose. Because of the accidents of history, many accounting developments took place in the US earlier than they did in the UK. Moreover, accounting became established as a university subject much more widely in the US, one result being a much greater volume and breadth of published writings on the subject. For this reason, in my interviews, I often asked about American influences on the respondent's thinking, and sought out who had been opinion leaders in their fields. I revisited controversial matters of accounting at many points, and these are explained in the next section for the benefit of readers who may not be familiar with them.

Key problem areas in accounting

Income

The purpose of a business entity is to supply goods or services from one period to the next. If the aim of the entity is to make a profit, its managers are judged mainly on the profits they make, subject to the current laws and conventions that constrain the way the firm deals with its various stakeholders such as employees, suppliers and customers.

There is an ambiguity attaching to the name 'income': does it refer to the level of sales revenue over the year, out of which all the costs of producing those sales must be met? Or does it refer only to the net profit, after meeting all the costs? Even the most basic concepts in accounting, as in economics, prove subtle and elusive when they are examined closely. Moreover, disagreements over the definition of assets, income, costs and profits can lead to controversy and misunderstandings. Some of the questions raised in the twelve interviews concern alternative ways to define and calculate profits, although always in the context of entities intended to make profits.

Conceptually, it is possible to think of income as being the difference between a set of assets at the start of the period and the corresponding set at the end. This is, indeed, how the UK's Accounting Standards Board tried to conceptualise income towards the end of the 20th century, some years after the interviews. There are serious difficulties with this. It is very hard to capture a comprehensive set of the assets of a firm (minus all its liabilities) at a particular date. Many assets are intangible, hard to value, and imprecisely defined. For example, the human skills and knowledge embodied in the workforce may represent a major resource - indeed, by far the most important in a professional firm - but firms do not own their staff. Moreover, assets are often written off in the accounts before they cease to be used, and assets may be constructed by the firm itself, rather than bought, so that their costs or values are not recorded at any exact figure.

Traditionally, accounting has proceeded by quite a different method. The assets and liabilities recorded in the books are those bought through historical transactions, and these provide the basis for an opening list of net assets, alongside the sources of capital that financed their acquisition, in the opening balance sheet. The assets do not purport to be a complete set, or to represent current values. The opening balance sheet may simply be seen as the closing balance sheet at the end of the preceding period. Then the income for the following year is calculated by totalling all the sales invoiced (both cash and credit sales) in the period, and then deducting the estimated costs of obtaining those sales, a process known as 'income recognition and cost matching'.

Note that the driver of this process is income recognition, determined by what has been invoiced to customers in the period. Invoices are written notices to customers to tell them that their account has been charged with the amount shown, which will be treated as a debt legally enforceable in the courts unless the customer challenges the facts as shown. The invoice date is not necessarily the date on which legal title to goods transfers. Invoices are usually sent when goods are dispatched, as a matter of good business practice, or when services have been rendered.

Estimating the cost of sales may present problems. Some costs are fairly clear-cut, such as the actual purchase price paid for each motor car sold by a car dealer. Others are less exact, mainly because there is no way to allocate joint costs between sales or time periods except on an arbitrary basis. Assume a lorry is bought for, say, £30,000 and used for five years. It is not evident how much of the £30,000 is 'used up' in any particular year. It is unreasonable to argue that the entire cost relates to the first year and so should be charged against sales revenues for that one year. The truck wears out, but not in any measurable way. It may perhaps be fair, in some sense, to assume that each year uses up £6,000 'worth' of the asset. It is safer to say that the whole £30,000 is used up over the whole 5 year period, but even this raises problems. In the earlier years of its life, who can predict how long the lorry is going to last, unless this is a policy choice made by the firm, regardless of the state of the vehicle in later years? It could be used for six or seven years. Furthermore, the actual cost of £30,000 might have been a stroke of luck, not representative of lorry costs generally. What if a replacement for the truck at the end of five years is expected to cost £50,000 - should the earlier years be charged with more than £6,000, in the expectation that it costs £10,000 per annum on average to be able to buy another truck five years later, to keep operations going? The problem of how to deal with changing prices is considered further in the next section.

Income recognition and cost matching became, over the centuries, the conventional way to calculate income, since it incorporated all the cash and credit transactions that the firm engaged in. These must be recorded in any case, to keep track of amounts owed by, and to, the firm. Each period ends with a process of year-end adjustments, in which the firm checks whether any costs relating to this period are not already recorded in the accounts. For example, certain components might already have been used for production even though the supplier has not yet sent an invoice for goods supplied on credit. And the process of averaging the depreciation of long-lived assets, such as the £30,000 lorry discussed earlier, means adjusting figures already recorded in the accounts. All twelve of the interviewees were, of course, very familiar with this system, and accepted it - subject to reservations over the treatment of changing prices. But they were also well aware of the problems of defining, and maintaining, capital, reporting income, and deciding how much could be paid out as dividends, in accordance with the law and with business prudence.

Changing prices

Given the timing of the interviews (1979 to 1984), it is not surprising that accounting for inflation often arose as an issue. The rate of inflation was high in the 1970s (induced by a sharp rise in crude oil prices from 1971). It was during the 1970s that the most turbulent arguments arose in Britain over whether to replace or augment the well established historical cost conventions by some system of inflation accounting, based either on current purchasing power or some variant of replacement cost accounting, both of which are discussed more fully below. Lawrence Robson and Jack Clayton both took strong positions that the only real solution to the problem of accounting for inflation was for government to stop inflation. Will Baxter supported replacement costs, and Harry Norris was notable because, however 'unlearned' the profession at the time, he wrote a most interesting and penetrating book on inflation accounting in the 1940s, working from first principles and with no university education.

To me, as one of the small number of accounting academics in UK universities in the early 1970s, inflation accounting was such a big issue that it virtually constituted the whole of 'accounting theory' at the time. I had come to favour some replacement cost solutions in the form of a mandatory supplementary statement to show how much, in the directors' judgment, would be needed as an additional charge against income to augment historical costs profits in order to maintain operating capacity intact.

During the period from 1850 to 1900 accounting rules were being developed to deal with the large numbers of companies formed under the new companies legislation. Throughout this half century prices in general were falling, which meant that income recognition using cost matching on the basis of the actual costs of inputs used (the 'historical cost' method) tended to show a relatively cautious picture of business performance. Input costs tended to fall from one period to the next, rather than rise. In the earlier example of the £30,000 truck, its replacement might cost, say, £20,000 rather than £50,000. So a system that matched replacement costs against revenues, rather than historical costs, would produce larger reported profit figures or smaller losses than the historical cost method.

By contrast, from 1900 to 1920 and from 1940 to 1950 prices rose rapidly due to large-scale international wars and the enormous diversion of industrial and commercial capacity to destructive ends. It rapidly became obvious, particularly to engineers and accountants working within large manufacturing firms, that if profits were reported on a historical cost basis, there was a serious risk that companies would be unable to maintain their operating capacity when the time came to replace major items of equipment - at least, without a need to raise fresh capital from shareholders or creditors.

Note that the converse problem did little harm. When prices fell, profits were lower under the prevailing historical cost than under an alternative replacement cost system. Company law required that dividends to shareholders could not exceed reported profits, so excess caution in calculating profits could limit the amount that owners could withdraw. This law was intended to protect creditors in the face of limited liability, since they could only recover their debts from the company itself, and not sue shareholders. But profit retention generally results in reinvestment and hence higher future profits, so that even if the rules for defining profit were excessively cautious, they would generally benefit creditors while doing no serious harm to the shareholders.

On the other hand, once price levels generally began to rise, historical cost tended to overstate profits as compared with replacement cost methods. If the firm could not replace its £30,000 truck after 5 years, it was failing to maintain its capital. Creditors would suffer from this lack of conservatism, and so indeed might shareholders if they were deceived by reports of overstated profit figures that failed to charge adequate amounts for inputs consumed. As noted earlier, the practical problem with depreciation charges on long-lived assets is to know how much to charge for the use of such assets, year by year, when both the length of their expected future life is unpredictable and so are their eventual replacement costs. Two solutions to the problem have been suggested. One uses replacements costs and the other applies index numbers to the original historical purchase prices of assets. Both methods were being advocated during the 20th century and are summarised below.

Replacement costs

Whereas future replacement costs are usually unpredictable, the current level of an asset's replacement cost can often be ascertained by looking to market prices quoted at the end of each year. Even this might not be easy. Technical changes in the nature of assets, such as trucks, can mean that older assets are outmoded. Furthermore, current (new) buying prices rarely reflect the second hand prices of assets actually owned. Moreover, some types of asset with specific and limited uses may well not be quoted at all on second-hand markets. There was also the problem that aggregate depreciation written off over the life of the asset would represent neither its original cost nor its ultimate replacement cost.

Other difficulties arise, too, such as the rate of technical change (assets are replaced by more efficient substitutes), as well as the difficulty of predicting asset lives (many fixed assets often continue to be used for twice the life originally estimated for them).

Two other complexities are worth noting. It is fairly obvious that rising asset prices mean that charging only the historical cost of assets against income will risk that the original assets cannot be replaced, but it is not clear how to test whether an adequate charge is being made. It is very difficult to know when some given level of operating capacity is being maintained at a constant level. What is it that needs to be observed? The crude number of assets is scarcely relevant, and their output capacity cannot be measured in any sensible way. Difficult judgements are needed before directors can say that they have charged enough against income to ensure that operating capital can be maintained intact. These issues are discussed in several of the interviews, particularly with the people who spent a career in industry. Thus, for example, Stanley Dixon was making practical use of replacement cost methods for decisions over pricing and output even though he was well aware that they needed judgement. Bill Fea, Lawrence Robson and Harry Norris all had extensive experience of the problems, although Norman Lancaster comments that fixed asset replacement was not a serious problem at Wolseley.

Deep controversy arose, also, over the question of whether monetary assets, such as cash, bank balances and debtors, needed to be maintained as well as non-monetary assets, such as inventories, machinery and goodwill. Orthodox accounting practice said that historical cost accounts gave a fair view of profits actually made in a period; if prices were rising, it would be prudent of directors to set aside some part of the reported profits to enable the firm to replace its assets. Calculating profits did not involve setting aside funds to use to replace assets, but merely charging the actual cost of the assets in use. There was no need to pre-judge whether assets would be in fact replaced at all at the end of their lives. Critics of this historical cost tradition insisted that historical cost did not give a fair view of profits.

Very similar debates over how to deal with inflation arose in Britain both in the 1940s and in the 1970s. During the 1970s, a variant of replacement cost accounting was devised that augmented historical cost charges by extra supplementary charges based on the current replacement cost of fixed assets and inventories, plus an amount to maintain the purchasing power of monetary assets. This system, known as 'Current Cost Accounting' or CCA, was complicated and it was greeted by most accountants without any great enthusiasm, although support was expressed in the interviews with Jack Clayton and also with Kenneth Wright and Harry Norris (who were both persuaded that this was better than the replacement cost method they had preferred previously). However, the many critics of historical cost accounting usually preferred some other method than current cost accounting of dealing with historical cost shortcomings.

Applying index numbers to a historical cost system

As an alternative to replacement cost accounting, some critics of the historical cost method argued that the main problem with historical cost was that the purchasing power of money itself fluctuated. The value of money rises with a fall in the general level of prices, and falls when prices on average go up. It is therefore possible to construct indices of asset prices, for the sorts of asset used by an individual firm, or within an industry category, or across the economy as a whole for all manufacturing and commercial businesses, or even for consumer prices. Such indices can be used to adjust historical cost figures so that they are all expressed, not in terms of their nominal money value, but in standardised units of the purchasing power of money.

Such a system is called a 'Current Purchasing Power' (or 'Constant Purchasing Power') method or CPP. At the end of each year, the reported accounting numbers are restated so that transactions recorded at earlier dates (when cash bought more, in an era of rising prices) are shown as re-measured by the larger number of year-end currency units needed to buy a similar amount at year-end prices. An intrinsic feature of such a system is that depreciation charges on long-lived assets are automatically restated to end-year price levels, and so also are monetary assets and liabilities held from earlier dates. The problem of 'backlog' is addressed automatically, and there is no need for any debate that monetary assets must be taken into consideration - they are re-valued as part of the system.

Two points are worth noting. One is that current purchasing power accounting was fully analysed earlier than replacement cost accounting, which tended to be developed in a more piecemeal manner. Thus, Henry Sweeney (1936) provided a detailed explanation of current purchasing power in the 1930s. It is also significant that current purchasing power came to be supported more strongly, both in the US and in the UK by standard setters, before rival replacement cost (or current cost accounting) systems were seriously considered. One reason for this was that current purchasing power could apply the same official sets of price indices to the historical cost accounts of a wide range of companies, so avoiding a lot of difficult judgments within individual companies. It limited scope for directors to manage the results to suit their preferences.

The second point is that current purchasing power replaces money units with constant purchasing power units, in just the same way that foreign currencies have to be translated into the domestic reporting currency of a company with branches or subsidiaries in foreign countries. But current purchasing power units do not necessarily have to be used only to restate historical cost accounts; they can in principle be used to restate replacement cost accounts too, although this tends to make a complex system even more difficult.

Because current purchasing power can use a small number of official indices, the method appealed to professional bodies that stressed the importance of verifiable processes that could be monitored, for example, by the auditors. But a small number of current purchasing power indices could arguably fail to satisfy the needs of particular individual companies whose asset prices moved out line with prices more generally (as built into the weighting of any individual index). For example, oil prices tend to be a relatively small component of the annual costs of many companies - even manufacturing companies that use energy for heat or light or transportation. But oil prices are of central importance to oil companies, a category which includes some of the largest companies in the world.

The engineers intuitively foresaw the problems of historical cost, which meant that companies might be unable to maintain their operating capacity intact, and were mainly concerned with the particular needs of their own company, not the economy in general. They knew about the replacement cost levels of the sorts of machines and materials that they used from day to day, not some abstract index published by a government department. Accountants serving the needs of major companies also identified with this problem, and tended to favour replacement cost approaches, although both Eric Hay Davison and Bill Fea used current purchasing power methods with specific indices in their companies. Davison, then at Courtaulds, gave a talk entitled 'Current Depreciation Problems of a large Industrial Undertaking' in November 1947, to one of the seminars on 'Problems in Industrial Administration', organised by Professor R. S. Edwards in the evenings at the London School of Economics. Accountants trained as auditors tended to favour current purchasing power, if they agreed that historical cost was inadequate. Eric Hay Davison discusses the issue at some length in his interview. In Mumford (1979), I analyse the UK debates over replacement cost and current purchasing power in the 1940s and 1970s.

Taxation

Governments have always raised taxes, mainly for warfare but also, since the Keynesian economic reforms of the mid-20th century, to help pursue social policies such as full employment. Levels of tax rose very sharply during the two World Wars, which were more heavily mechanised than previous conflicts. Accountants were called upon by the UK government to help in the war effort, mainly in administration such as the production of munitions and weaponry but also, just as critically, in the administration of taxation.

New taxes were imposed, partly to raise funds and also, by way of excess profits levies, to penalise profiteering from the war. The most important source of revenue was personal income tax, and tax rates were set at levels that approached 98% for certain high levels of 'unearned' income. Accounts needed to be reliable and as fair as possible, but for tax payers there were increasing incentives to obtain the best possible tax advice. Tax policies and their implementation required a huge increase in skilled staff, particularly since many policies involved expert judgement over what constituted transactions, income, expenses and so on. Unusually, the figure of income used as the basis for tax assessments in the UK, in contrast, say, with Germany, does not have to be the figure published as income in the accounts. Accounting profits are subject to various adjustments for the tax assessment, laid down in tax law and regarded as part of private negotiations between taxpayer and the Inland Revenue. Thus, depreciation on long-lived assets is a policy matter for the directors to decide upon, but rates at which the costs of fixed assets are allowed to be deducted for tax are laid down separately in tax statutes.

Another unusual feature of British public affairs is that taxation is mainly left to accountants rather than lawyers, as is generally the case elsewhere. Thus, accountants usually prepare and submit tax returns in the UK for wealthy individuals and companies, and their professional training includes taxation. Firms of accountants in public practice often rely on taxation for a significant part of their revenues, and have specialist partners who oversee that part of the firm's work. Amongst those I interviewed, Bruce Sutherland was a tax specialist, and Kenneth Wright was very knowledgeable; however, one of the industrial accountants, Jack Clayton, played a singularly important role in UK tax administration. Personal income tax before the 1940s involved an assessment at the end of each tax year of the amount of income tax payable, which then had to be paid over in the course of the next year or two. In the 1940s, Paul Chambers at the Board of Inland Revenue set up a team to develop a system of 'pay-as-you-earn' (PAYE) taxation, so that employees would have tax deducted weekly at source by employers from their pay. Jack Clayton was sometimes given credit for devising PAYE, but in his interview it is clear that he only suggested modifications to the system that was being proposed by Paul Chambers.

The interviews reflect the specialised nature of tax in the UK because, even though all those interviewed had studied taxation for their professional examinations, most of the twelve interviewees claimed no expert knowledge of the field.

Group accounts

The techniques of accounting developed, to a large extent, in response to institutional developments. For example, 'consolidated accounts' for groups of companies developed in the US, because the need grew there first. Until 1890, it was illegal for one American company to own shares in another, but the Sherman Anti-Trust Act permitted the practice from that date, so that it became possible for one company to take control of another by buying a majority of its voting share capital.

Buying all the shares in a company gives the acquirer complete control over it, but rather than liquidating the target, as generally happened in the UK after a takeover, the new parent often kept the other in existence as a subsidiary. But merely showing the cost price of the investment in its accounts gave little idea of how significant the operating assets were that were now under the parent's control. The new technique of consolidation accounting developed to show a group's entire assets and liabilities together, as if they were those of a single legal entity.

The group company structure became commonplace in the US after 1900, making it possible for investors to build up pyramids of control with less than 100% ownership (Bonbright and Means, 1932). Preparing consolidated accounts was a brilliant new device. It seems to have been devised and installed originally by J. P. Morgan for the new giant groups that the bank was then forming, such as Federal Steel Company soon to become, in 1901, the core of the United States Steel Company, with the first balance sheet showing $1,000 millions in assets and audited by Price Waterhouse. It should be noted that the claim, such as that by Allen and McDermott (1993), that the auditors and A. L. Dickinson specifically devised the technique seems somewhat exaggerated. Stock market investors were impressed, even though it came to be shown later that much of the value on display in these consolidated balance sheets consisted of notional goodwill (Walker, 1978).

There were some difficult problems to resolve in the new technique of group accounts. For example, the group balance sheet aggregated all the cash, bank balances and debtors belonging to all the companies in the group, and all the external liabilities owed to creditors. But, as a matter of law, each company was a separate legal entity, regardless of who owned its share capital, so the creditors of a subsidiary company could only sue the subsidiary to recover their debts, not the group as a whole. To this extent, critics argued, group accounts were misleading. Of course, the subsidiaries would have to prepare their own separate accounts, and creditors needed to rely on those rather than the group accounts. Debts owed by one company to another in the group needed to be cancelled out, so that aggregate group indebtedness was not overstated. Inventory valuations also needed to be adjusted to remove any profits realised on sales from one company to another in the group but not realised by sale outside the group.

Moreover, where a parent owned less than 100% of a subsidiary's shares, the question arose of how to treat the minority of shares not owned by the group, say, for illustration, 10%. One possibility was for the group accounts only to bring in 90% of the subsidiary's assets and liabilities, taking the view that the other 10% belonged to the minority shareholders. This, however, was unrealistic. Either the parent controlled all the subsidiary or it did not. So the practice grew of showing 100% of the assets and liabilities in the group accounts and also, as a special form of group liability, the amounts owed to minority shareholders in the subsidiaries. This represented the capital they owned, plus their entitlement to any profits of the subsidiary not yet distributed as dividends.

Although, as explained, the technique of group accounting developed in the US, before there was any legal compulsion to do so, it was used in the UK from the 1920s, also on a voluntary basis. The 1929 UK Companies Act required group accounts to be prepared, but left such a large loophole that they were rarely prepared in practice. It was not until the 1947 Companies Act, consolidated in the 1948 Companies Act, that group accounts were effectively made compulsory. Even then, the area has remained problematic, particularly over the criteria used to define when one company controls another. Bill Fea, in his interview, refers to the problems of consolidating the accounts of the GKN group.

Accounting standards

However, group accounts are not the only area of difficulty. Many details of accounting policy offer scope for companies and, of course, unincorporated entities such as sole trading concerns, partnerships and many charities to use different treatments for similar items. Depreciation on long-lived assets is just one such area of policy. The valuation of inventories can also present a variety of treatments; for example, a manufacturing company can decide how much of the indirect costs to include in the value of any one year's production costs. It was to achieve uniformity of treatment, and hence a better comparability, that accountants from the mid-20th century began to consider the need for standardised treatments, whether on a voluntary or a compulsory basis.

The Wall Street crash of 1929 in the US was much more severe than the corresponding stock market falls in Europe and the UK. In 1933 and 1934, federal legislation followed in America that was much more dramatic than anything in Europe, and included the creation of the Securities and Exchange Commission (SEC) to regulate the market for quoted companies. The SEC was formally charged with the task of drawing up detailed rules for accounting disclosure, but leaders of the accounting profession (led by George O. May, senior partner in Price Waterhouse, New York, a naturalised immigrant from England) persuaded the SEC to delegate this task of setting accounting standards to the American Institute of Accountants. It is notable that George May figures in the interviews with Kenneth Wright, Eric Davison, Jack Clayton, William Fea and Will Baxter. However, the SEC, since its inception, has always retained an important role in monitoring accounting standards as well as the accounts filed by individual companies with the stock exchanges. Detailed mandatory accounting standards were, thus, being set in the US from the mid-1930s.

In Britain, the ICAEW set up its own programme of Recommendations on Accounting Principles from 1942. These had persuasive influence but no legal backing. The roles of accounting standards were quite different in the two countries. Within the UK, company law since 1844 had required accounts to be prepared for members and also filed on public record with the Registrar of Companies, but the law said little about the detailed contents of the accounts. The Recommendations on Accounting Principles were intended to standardise the treatment of controversial items for all companies - not just listed companies as in the US. The SEC, by contrast, has always had the force of government behind it, and could refuse permission for accounts to be filed with the stock exchanges - without which their securities would be suspended from quotation. Thus, while the SEC's authority only extended to quoted companies, rather than the great majority of unquoted smaller ones, US accounting standards had a degree of legal backing that was lacking in the UK.

During the Second World War in Britain, there were strong pressures for accountants to contribute to public policy making, and close relationships built up between the UK professional accountancy bodies and various parts of government (see, for example, Noguchi and Edwards, 2004). Reference is made to this cooperation in several of the interviews; for example, Fea notes the advice needed from GKN to make consolidated group accounts work in practice. Professions in general had grown over the centuries out of a tradition of expert service to the community, by claiming a right to privileged control over areas of practice that often involved a monopoly of practising rights as well as restricted access to training and certification. Within the UK, professional bodies of accountants developed from the early 19th century, with a great deal of lobbying by them, to be recognised in law to take appointments to various forms of public office, for example to administer bankrupt estates, to audit public bodies and companies, and later to give independent financial advice (Stacey, 1951). Six major UK accountancy bodies emerged from the campaigns of the 20th century, together with a handful of other bodies that have won lesser recognition and status.

Many accountants served in the Second World War in the armed forces, and hundreds lost their lives in the process. Many others were exempted from military service in view of the value of their work to the national administration and to the economic output of the nation. At the end of the war, thousands of accountants returned to civilian life, and ICAEW in particular set up series of lectures to help its members to adjust to work in a post-war Britain beset with a plethora of regulations, taxes, rationing and austerity. All twelve interviewees refer to these lectures, which clearly influenced their relationships with the profession and with each other. Thus, Kenneth Wright refers to the ICAEW as being remote from its members until the lecture courses were organised. The ICAEW itself was very short of resources after 1945, yet members agreed voluntarily to raise their membership subscriptions in several successive years in order to help it out. Morale amongst members was raised to a rare degree because of this involvement in the lecture series.

Post-war recovery saw a gradual rise in living standards, economic growth, and a slow freeing of business from many of the regulations that the war had necessitated. From time to time, financial scandals upset investor confidence, and these tended to raise doubts about the efficacy of accounting and auditing processes. Business became much more international as trade and foreign investment grew. Competition grew, too, as mainland European countries rebuilt their industries and challenged the economic power which the Americans had established since the 1890s and had expanded during the war years.

Serious questions over accounting rules arose in particular towards the end of the 1960s, widely publicised in the UK press (Stamp and Marley, 1970). For example, the Accounting Standards Steering Committee was set up in the UK in 1970, largely in response to the prompting of Eddie Stamp, with the task of restoring confidence in financial markets just as US legislation had sought to do after the Wall Street Crash. By the dates of my interviews, a number of standards had been issued, with the backing of the six major professional bodies of accountants, some of them readily accepted and uncontroversial but others only after fierce debate.

I was teaching the contents of these SSAPs in the classroom, and I was also involved in discussing them within my professional body (then the Association of Certified and Corporate Accountants, and now the Association of Chartered Certified Accountants). Accounting standards were still relatively recent in the UK, and there was still a sense that they were 'owned' by the profession rather than being imposed by a separate authoritative body. Until 1990, SSAPs had to be adopted by the professional bodies to give them authority. The standard setting body could not demand enforcement since UK law declined to back them specifically. In fact, the Companies Acts only required that the accounts showed a 'true and fair' view, without setting out what this meant in practice.

Accounting for tax was one of the areas of difficulty. UK standard setters had adopted a US approach that treated taxes as an expense of running the business. This ran counter to traditional British views of tax as an appropriation of part of the profits of the business, rather than a charge necessary to the process of earning profits. After all, no tax was paid at all unless there were profits.

The most controversial issue of all was how to deal with inflation. As noted earlier, some accountants were content still to use historical cost accounting, whilst others preferred current purchasing power adjustments to the historical cost accounts, and those in industry and commerce typically wanted a replacement cost system, particularly if this meant profits could be reduced for the purposes of tax assessments. Given that several of the accountants interviewed had made their careers in industry, they might be expected to favour replacement cost accounting. Indeed, some of them expressed a lot of sympathy with this view. But all of them had trained as chartered accountants in auditing offices, and they all appreciated the need for accounting to be verifiable and orderly. Moreover, they tended to accept that the main duty of a company was to serve the interests of its shareholders, although it was notable how strongly some of them, like Norman Lancaster, expressed their loyalty to employees, and sought to keep them informed of what was going on in the business. Some, particularly Lawrence Robson, Bruce Sutherland and Jack Clayton, were uneasy about inflation accounting on the grounds that it implied an acceptance of inflation at a time when government should be under the greatest possible pressure to reduce the causes of inflation.

An important message from the interviews was that even this group of accountants, who took an unusually active part in the affairs of the profession, owed their prime loyalty to their employers. Most worked for large companies, and served their employers with commitment and dedication whilst also 'doing their bit' for the profession. They seemed to have enjoyed their work and derived great satisfaction from doing it well. They spent relatively little time on tax and legal compliance and more on financial and managerial systems to guide decisions, to raise capital, and optimise the efficient usage of resources.

Costing

Within companies, accountants began to develop operational control systems from the late 19th century, led once again by American practice because of the much larger size of US companies and the more advanced professional training of American managers. For example, as early as 1900, MBA degrees were starting to become a common feature of the education of managers in the US whatever their specialist backgrounds, so that for example a production engineer would learn something about marketing, finance and business strategy as well as further engineering skills. MBAs were often studied on a part-time basis at evening classes at many American universities.

In Britain, it was much rarer for business managers to take any formal qualifications, and universities were much slower to offer business-related degrees. Indeed, one of the reasons why there were very many more qualified accountants in Britain than in other countries (per head of population) was that accountancy represented one of the few available means by which to obtain a formal business qualification. Few accountants until the 1970s had degrees, and far fewer had degrees in accounting, but they could study part-time, mainly through correspondence courses, to obtain their qualification as a chartered accountant or as a certified or cost accountant.

The nature of cost accounting changed very dramatically during the 20th century. Accumulating data to make up the costs of production typically involved large numbers of items being recorded, collected, tabulated and added. This was clerical work in the early days, and cost accounting was very much a matter of managing large staffs of clerks (often women, even before women were employed in large numbers outside millwork).

The mechanisation of data collection and processing began with adding machines and progressed to punched card equipment until computers took over data processing. The ability of computers to rapidly re-analyse large amounts of data enabled alternative forms of analysis to be calculated very fast and at relatively low cost, and it soon became possible to transmit information over electronic networks. This facility much increased once the internet became available - but this was after the time of my interviews.

Accounting involves accessing and reporting on every part of an organisation, and the accountant typically manages the process of setting budget forecasts as well as reporting actual outcomes in relation to those budgets. The accounting team is thus very well positioned strategically to know the organisation and how it functions. The development of standard cost accounting, once again mainly in the US, grew wherever the business involved repeated, standardised activities. Standard amounts of inputs were identified as necessary to perform each major function, and production staff were held responsible for using such inputs efficiently, at pre-set standard price rates. Purchasing budgets were usually the responsibility of specialist buying departments, who would be held responsible for variations between standard and actual prices, just as the production staff were responsible for variations between standard and actual quantities of inputs used. Norman Lancaster gave a lecture on 'Budgeting and Standard Costs in the Engineering Industry' in February

1950 to one of Ronnie Edwards' industrial administration seminars, and both Bill Fea and Jack Clayton speak of their importance.

It was about the time of the interviews, from 1979 onwards, that even standardised operations started to become less suited to standard costing. Greater flexibility in production, as well as fuller delegation of control to operating units, led to control by means of financial targets set in much less detail than the full standard costing systems. At their fullest, standard costing systems were often integrated with the financial accounting system to produce, as a by-product, inventory reports on raw materials, work in progress and finished stocks as well as the costs of goods actually sold in each period.

New debates arose over the best ways in which complex multi-unit organisations could be controlled, but there were inherent tensions between delegating authority to line managers to make decisions and centralising decisions to achieve optimal results for the group as a whole. In this area, as in others, like how to allocate joint costs, there was no correct answer waiting to be discovered, although many people tried to discover one.

Summary of key issues

The UK accountancy profession was described earlier as being 'unlearned'. I hope that this brief review of some of the key problem areas in accounting shows why it is that accounting is not a precise discipline, with a set of definitive solutions for any situation. It requires judgment to address the complexities of organisational life, with all the behavioural subtleties than control systems involve. The people I interviewed had ample experience of accounting complexities in practice. Those who spent their working lives in auditing practice were closely attuned to the needs of their clients, whilst those who worked in industry were aware of the needs of their companies for sound business strategies and good team relations with their colleagues and employees.

Introducing the twelve people interviewed

The introductions, like the transcripts that follow, are presented here in chronological order of the interviews. The reason is that several passages in the interviews make reference to people who were interviewed later, and about whom I knew little at the time. There is no order of seniority here, the order often being a matter of luck, determined, for example, by when people happened to be free to give me time to visit them. Only the interviews with Kenneth Wright, Jack Clayton, Basil Smallpeice and Bruce Sutherland are published here in book form, this group comprising an important and diverse sub-set of the group. The interviews with the other eight are all available on the website of the Institute of Chartered Accountants of Scotland - www.icas.org.uk/research

This selection of interviewees is biased by the inclusion of relatively few people in auditing practice and a lot of people with industrial careers. This is largely because patterns of audit practice are more similar than the preoccupations of industrial accountants. Thus, the sorts of issue that Stanley Dixon discusses are mainly to do with how to set costs and prices for chemical products where most distillation processes are common to all of them. It hardly mattered in some respects which products were regarded as the principal products of tar distilling and which the by-products. The output proportions could not be changed very readily, even if selling prices made some more profitable than others. Basil Smallpeice, by contrast, was mainly concerned with high level business strategy, in BOAC and later in Cunard. His work did not require accounting skills as much as a very high level of managerial skills. Even so, his autobiography (Smallpeice, 1981), published, as it happens, within months of my interview with him, makes frequent reference to contribution margins and similar concepts very familiar to accountants, and these were very valuable in the task of putting resources to their most useful applications.

E. Kenneth Wright

Kenneth Wright spent his entire working life in practice, becoming senior partner in Dearden Farrow (now part of BDO Stoy Hayward). This was not one of the largest international firms, but a substantial firm nevertheless, with its head office in London and a number of offices in other cities. He refers in the interview to his impaired hearing, but he was an excellent communicator, with a pronounced sense of humour. As noted earlier, he stressed the meticulous care with which the ICAEW set about planning its merger with the Society of Incorporated Accountants and Auditors, after the two presidents had talked over such a scheme on a transatlantic voyage to New York. Kenneth Wright was one of the fairly small number of graduates taken into articles before the Second World War, having read economics at Cambridge. He qualified as a chartered accountant in 1933, and became president of the ICAEW in 1975. His studies in economics gave him sympathy with the use of replacement costs as a solution to accounting for inflation, although, as the interview shows, he later came to regard current purchasing power accounting as preferable.

Lawrence W. Robson (interview available in electronic form only)

Although he was a practising accountant throughout his career, founding a substantial and successful auditing firm in Robson Rhodes, Lawrence Robson was just as much committed to management consultancy and he founded a second firm - Robson Morrow - which also flourished. He had a flair for marketing his ideas, his firms, and himself. He did not attend university, entering articles at the age of 16, and joining Peat Marwick (now KPMG) after qualifying as a chartered accountant in 1929. He quickly developed a reputation as a problem solver during the Second World War, and he led one of the delegations that visited the United States under the Marshall Plan to re-build British industry once the war finished. He drafted a text for the ICAEW on standard costing that became one of the major primers on the subject. He also took an active interest in public affairs, and held office in the Liberal Party.

Stanley Dixon (interview available in electronic form only)

A graduate of Oxford in classics, philosophy and ancient history, Stanley Dixon qualified with a small firm in 1927 and then joined Peat Marwick. He soon decided to follow a career in industry, as did the majority of chartered accountants by the middle of the 20th century, and he spent his career with Yorkshire Midland Tar Distillers in the English Midlands. He retained an interest in the affairs of the ICAEW, and joined first the Birmingham and District Society, and then the ICAEW Council in 1958. He was the first president of the ICAEW to come from industry. Until the late 1940s, the ICAEW's Council was only open to members who were 'principals' (partners or sole practitioners, rather than employees) in auditing firms. While several of the other people interviewed (e.g. Eric Davison, Basil Smallpeice and Jack Clayton) were heavily involved in campaigns to change this policy, Dixon was not an active campaigner, and by the time he joined Council attitudes had already changed. Much of the interview was about the nature of his company's business, and dealing with joint costs. He used replacement costs within the company, but not for financial reporting under the Companies Act.

Eric Hay Davison (interview available in electronic form only)

Another non-graduate, Eric Hay Davison qualified in 1928 with a medium-sized firm and went into industry shortly afterwards, first with HMV at Hayes, Middlesex, then at Turner Brothers in Rochdale, then back to London with Simpson's, Courtaulds and GEC. From the 1930s, in London, he became involved with some important institutional developments, notably the creation of the Accounting Research Association (which foundered after the war), and later with both the London Society of Chartered Accountants and the London Industrial Chartered Accountants Group (LICAG). He was one of the first non-practising members of the ICAEW Council (a chartered accountant who was not a partner or sole practitioner in a firm of practising auditors). His son, Ian, has also become a very well known member of the profession.

Jack Clayton

Jack Clayton came from Manchester, and qualified with a small firm in 1928 without taking a university degree. On qualifying with the ICAEW, he joined the leading Scottish auditing firm, Thomson McLintock (later absorbed into KPMG), in their Manchester office before going on to an industrial career. His experience with the construction industry led to his involvement with the development of the 'pay-as-you-earn' system of income tax. Always a vigorous campaigner and vocal critic, he became a member of ICAEW Council in 1948 and chair of its Taxation and Financial Relations Committee almost immediately. Although his career was mostly in commerce, he continued to play an active part in the deliberations of the profession, writing many articles and letters to the press and to the journals *The Accountant* and *Accountancy*. Both journals were privately owned and managed, but maintained close relationships with the ICAEW and often expressed views of the ICAEW Council. Despite his reputation for being hostile to inflation accounting, Jack Clayton makes clear in his interview his support for current cost accounting as developed by the 1975 Sandilands Committee on Accounting for Inflation. He was also keen on merging the main UK professional accountancy bodies into a single 'Royal Institute of Chartered Accountants'. He gave the impression of being a man very confident in his abilities, and it is easy to infer from the interview that he had an interest in receiving an honorary degree from Lancaster.

Norman G. Lancaster (interview available in electronic form only)

Another non-graduate, Norman Lancaster qualified in 1930 with a medium-sized auditing firm and then joined Deloittes. He was one of several of those interviewed who took up an industrial career in the English Midlands, rather more in a senior management capacity than in an accounting role. He was never a member of the ICAEW Council, but served on various committees, such as the Cost Accounting Sub-Committee. He expressed a view in the interview that it was important to have an accountant as number two or three in the management team, but preferably not as chief executive. He said he was disappointed to learn that GKN had recently appointed an accountant, Trevor Holdsworth, rather than an engineer, as chief executive of what was the largest engineering company in Britain. When Bill Fea read of this, he told me in correspondence that he was heavily involved in securing the appointment of Trevor Holdsworth to GKN - where Fea himself spent most of his career - it was 'probably the best thing I ever did in my life'. Amongst Norman Lancaster's interests was the University of Birmingham, on whose finance committee he served and from whom - like Stanley Dixon - he received an honorary doctorate.

Sir Basil Smallpeice

Sir Basil Smallpeice graduated with a B Com degree from London University as an external student, and qualified in 1930 with a small firm, moving from Norwich to London with them after his first year as a trainee. Immediately on qualifying he moved into industry, where he spent his whole career, latterly in very senior positions in British Overseas

Airways Corporation (later merged with British European Airways to form British Airways) and then the Cunard steamship company. In both, he was heavily involved in rescuing a major transport business that was in serious financial difficulties, and restoring each of them to health. To his evident chagrin, he was dismissed in each case soon after the business had been rescued, in the case of BOAC as a political decision by the Conservative government of the time, and in the case of Cunard after the takeover by P&O (the Peninsular and Oriental line). His autobiography (Smallpeice, 1981) augments the interview valuably, but makes little reference to accountancy. He was a co-founder of the Accounting Research Association. He makes some critical comments about Lawrence Robson's understanding of standard costing, in which Smallpeice was well versed from his earlier days at Royal Doulton. He was author of a very influential paper, 'The Future of Auditing', during the Second World War which led to a major campaign to raise the profile of non-practising members of the ICAEW (debated at the ICAEW's Annual General Meetings in 1941 and 1942). He became the first non-practising member to become a member of the ICAEW Council.

William W. Fea (interview available in electronic form only)

An Oxford graduate in politics, economics and philosophy, Bill Fea qualified in 1931 with a small firm and soon went into industry where he made his career with Guest, Keen and Nettlefold (GKN), the major engineering conglomerate in the UK. He became a member of the ICAEW Council in 1948, chairing the Taxation and Financial Relations Committee. He supported the use of current purchasing power accounting, which he used at GKN, and he served on three successive ICAEW working parties on inflation accounting, one of which he chaired. He was also much occupied with introducing consolidated accounts at GKN, consisting of a group of 100 companies, and he was a member of the working party that worked on consolidation principles at the ICAEW in the course of advising on the group accounting requirements of the 1947 Companies Act. The ICAEW set up its Non-Practising Members' Committee in 1943, in response to the criticisms made by Basil Smallpeice and others, and Bill Fea was appointed as its first chair.

Bruce Sutherland

Unusually in this group of twelve, Sutherland specialised in taxation - he is still running his own practice in the Cotswolds. He served as an army officer in India until 1947, when he returned to England. He was then admitted to Nottingham University to read classics, but left after one year. He expresses in the interview a regret that he was not able to take up degree studies at Harvard, which he visited on a scholarship, after qualifying in 1951 with a medium-sized Midlands practice. Like Lawrence Robson and Jack Clayton, he took a keen interest in national politics, and held strong views about the need for government to control inflation by monetary policy. Unlike Lawrence Robson (an active member of the Liberal Party), Bruce Sutherland was a Conservative, strongly supportive of Margaret Thatcher. He was hostile both to inflation accounting and to accounting standards, and he also campaigned vigorously and effectively against merging professional accounting bodies.

Professor William T. Baxter (interview available in electronic form only)

The only Scot in the group, Will Baxter took his B Com at The University of Edinburgh and qualified as a Scottish Chartered Accountant with ICAS, with a small practice in that city in 1930 before entering a teaching career. He taught first in London, and then in Cape Town for several years before returning to London in 1947 to teach at the London School of Economics (LSE) until his retirement. He died in 2006, a month before a symposium at the LSE arranged to mark his attaining the age of 100. A more recent interview with him by Professor Geoffrey Whittington, published in an ICAS volume of interviews with four eminent Scottish accountants (Walker, 2005), augments the present interview. For many years, the accounting degrees at the LSE were the best known in the UK, with a three year undergraduate course and a Master's programme in the subject taught over two years (with exemption from the first year for those with a good honours first degree in a cognate subject). While the first UK accounting degrees were offered at Birmingham from 1902, the LSE followed soon afterwards, both taught by part-time staff. Will Baxter was the first full-time professor of accounting in England, and he continued to write long after his retirement from teaching. The history of academic accounting in the UK is vividly recounted in the *British Accounting Review* Special Edition in June 1997; particularly valuable in the present context are the papers by Stephen Zeff on the period from 1947-1959 and by Robert Parker on 1960-1971. Will Baxter was a prominent advocate of replacement cost accounting, although during the 1940s he supported constant purchasing power accounting.

Harry Norris (interview available in electronic form only)

Another non-graduate, Harry Norris qualified in 1934 with a small firm in Manchester, and then joined Deloittes in London before moving into industry. The major part of his career was spent with a major construction group, Wimpey, in the London area, and although he was not a member of the ICAEW's Council, he joined the Taxation and Financial Relations Committee as well as being an active member of LICAG. He was the main instigator of the joint working party on the definition of profits set up by the ICAEW and the National Institute for Economic and Social Research, which reported in 1946. The report served, unfortunately, to show how little economists and accountants understood one another in those days. I sought to contrast this schism with the closer understanding shown between *The Economist* Intelligence Unit and the ACCA a few years later (Mumford, 1983). Harry Norris wrote a book on inflation accounting, published in 1947, that made a strong case for a replacement cost system. He evidently also did some part-time teaching at the LSE.

Godfrey Judd (interview available in electronic form only)

Another practising accountant, Godfrey Judd (like Kenneth Wright) was an economics graduate from Cambridge before he joined his father's practice. Mann Judd was already a substantial firm, originally in Scotland but from the time of the First World War, it moved its main office to London. Godfrey Judd qualified in 1936, became a member of The 1949 Group that grew out of the ICAEW's Oxford Summer Schools, and became a member of the ICAEW's Council in 1967, as well as a member of a number of its committees (although not of T&FR). He went to America in 1952 as part of the Anglo-American Productivity year. The interview is interesting in part for its account of the history of Mann Judd before it disappeared (by merger or takeover) into Touche Ross, including the abrupt ending of Mann Judd's working relationship with Barrow Wade Guthrie in New York. This history can be compared with the short set of essays published privately by Mann Judd Gordon & Company (1967), to mark the 150th anniversary of the founding of the firm.

Postscript

The transcripts of these eminent accountants provide a rich set of source materials about the key issues that faced accountants in the middle of the 20th century and, indeed, that still face them today. Lively debate over particular problems has been an integral part of the profession, and it is clear from the interviews how engaged members of the Summer Schools, the LICAG and The 1949 Group became in their discussions. I hope that, by getting to know something about the people interviewed in this set of transcripts, the reader will come to appreciate more about the development of the economic and social roles of accountancy, and be encouraged to take an active part in helping the profession to carry forward its skills and knowledge in future.

E. KENNETH WRIGHT
INTERVIEWED BY
MICHAEL MUMFORD

27th March 1979 at the Reform Club, London

Let me first set the scene for a moment or two. I started in 1933, and I think if there is one thing that should be said about those days it is 'pity my simplicity!', because then accounting was a very much simpler affair than it has become since. We were only ten years away from the *Royal Mail Steam Packet* case, and a young man called Gilbert Garnsey had aroused great derision and contempt from everybody, except I think *The Economist* newspaper, when he gave a talk in 1932 about the need for bringing together the accounts of a company (which he called 'a parent company') and the companies that it owned (which he called 'its wholly owned subsidiaries'). And he called the exercise 'consolidated accounts'.

Well, that was 1932. And so in 1933 we were not very far out of the 'Dark Ages'; and as I remember accounting in those days, we were very much concerned with the detailed examination of historical records. Even with big companies like the Roan Antelope Copper Mines, I remember, or the diamond mines in West Africa, Selection Trust, or Chinese Engineering which owned mines in China, the work of the audit and work of accountant very largely consisted of making certain that the voluminous flow of information was correctly recorded in books, and that cash had gone into the bank, and so forth.

There was nothing in the form of a manual beyond what we used to call in those days 'an audit programme'; and for a fairly major audit, running in those days to £700 or £800 (which was very big money indeed in 1935) the audit programme for such a job would only be about three or four pages long. And so we went along in the 1930s, with one eye on Hitler. And the war came.

At that time, the Institute [Institute of Chartered Accountants in England and Wales, ICAEW] was to me, and I think to most other people, quite remote from the ordinary life of the members. It did not take any paternal interest in their affairs, and it was largely an examination and a disciplinary body. I think that has been expounded on many occasions. The only thing the Institute did with its members was an autumnal conference which was held biennially and attended by about 300 of the top accountants and their wives, at suitable seaside resorts around England. That did have the merit of bringing together at least some small part of the profession.

I think at that time there were about four to five thousand chartered accountants altogether. It goes without saying that entry into the profession in those days was by selection and the payment of a premium. It was the old-fashioned apprenticeship scheme. Quite literally, one worked under the senior partner. It cost him nothing; indeed, he had money for keeping you. And in my case at least he took his responsibility seriously. For example, he would come out every Thursday afternoon to a fairly big audit I was on for the best part of six or nine months, and the chief accountants and the directors would come into the room with their problems and he would discuss them quite openly, and I was able to sit there - and, since I was being paid I think £35 a year, he didn't worry that I was not earning any money for him during that time (although I dare say he charged out the number of hours I sat there to the clients).

So it was a more leisurely way. But it was what you probably regard with some derision as learning by 'sitting next to Nellie'.

Which firm were you with then?

This was Annan Dexter - the famous Annan Dexter of *Apfel versus Annan Dexter*, in those days a firm of four partners and a staff of about sixty, doing quite a wide range of jobs. In those days a small firm could do a wide range of jobs. We did, for example, the Lancashire Electric Power Company audit - a very big audit; the Cornish Electricity audit; and similarly some of the other electricity audits. And mines; in Yugoslavia, the Tretche Mines, now of course nationalised; a mine in Russia; and many, many mines in Africa: Roan Antelope, Sierra Leone Selection Trust diamond mine, Broken Hill Proprietary Mines in Northern Rhodesia - we did all those, although we were such a small firm.

So you had a specialisation?

No specialisation at all, really. I suppose audits were about 75% of the practice, but we also had a pretty substantial liquidation and receivership side, which was extremely good experience. I was the senior partner's 'favourite son' for a year or two and ran all the receiverships on his behalf, which was the greatest possible fun.

However, I think that most firms were rather similar in those days, even the great big ones. You had the partners themselves directly involved in the field work - in the audits, with the clients, face to face. A minimum of administration. There was some specialisation on tax, but even then tax was mainly straight-forward income tax, with the Five Schedules. There was a terrific row in 1937 when Neville Chamberlain introduced the National Defence Contribution at 4% for partners and 5% for corporations - that was the first break away.

In parenthesis at this stage, looking at the future, a great deal of my professional life was taken up with taxation, and I think that was the first big breach, which has led to all sorts of troubles. This is pure heresy on my part, but I believe in the end that tax is borne by an individual. I don't think something impersonal like a corporation or an institution 'bears tax'. 'Bears' in an emotive word meaning 'suffers', and the whole structure of income tax from 1803 onwards was on the footing that at the end of the line it was going to be borne by an individual. So the National Defence Contribution [NDC] was the first breach in the dam. A corporation was regarded merely as an agent for its shareholders. It was a joint venture - *The English Sewing Cotton* case (1830, or something like that - 1870?). The NDC opened the way, which of course was succeeded by Excess Profits Duty and Excess Profits Tax during the war. And gradually you began to think of the company as something quite separate from its owners, and then it developed of course into Corporation Tax now, and there was something in between - a Profits Tax and Special Levies and things like that. Losing that single straight core, that tax is on an individual, has led to all the complications.

The deferred tax proposals and this sort of thing?

Yes.

Well, going back to the Institute, the war came, and everything went on to a minor key, with one exception. I suppose many hundreds, if not thousands, of qualified chartered accountants went into the Forces. The Reserved Age was 30 upwards, so all qualified people under 30 went into the Forces and quite a number went into voluntarily above that age.

But among those who remained, there was a group of individuals who were interested in the theory of the thing, and in the long nights of night-watching, with bombs falling and that kind of thing, they formed something called 'The Taxation and Financial Relations Committee', the 'T&FR Committee', which in my view did an enormous job for the Institute. There were probably seven or eight of them; they were much senior to me. I should think probably the most senior of them was Sir Thomas Robson, who is still alive, the senior Past President of the Institute. And there would be Sir William Carrington, a Lancashire man, who would be more on the tax side. There was P. M. Rees (Peter Rees, Chief Accountant of Unilever - probably one the first industrial accountants to concern himself with the affairs of the Institute). There was Jack Clayton, a firebrand from one of the civil engineering companies, who incidentally invented P.A.Y.E.

And there was Sir William Lawson, senior partner of Binder Hamlyn. A little later on, Leonard Barrows of Birmingham. Bertram Nelson was not in it in those days because Bertram was doing similar sorts of thing in those days with the Society [of Incorporate Accountants and Auditors]: we had not yet joined up. And these people formed the T&FR committee. And there was also de Paula. De Paula greeted me at the first course I went to after the war. De Paula had picked up this lecture by the unknown man Gilbert Garnsey in 1932, and had gone back and had produced the Dunlop Rubber Co. accounts - the first consolidated accounts [in the UK] - in 1933/34.

They [the T&FR Committee] began to say that they ought to formalise a lot of the principles on which the profession was working, and they produced a whole range of Recommendations, which I think were very good. I think they were straightforward; they were simple. They did beg a lot of questions because even in those days there was controversy between the industrial and the other accountants, and quite a lot of people still wanted profits to be as long as a piece of string - as they still do. But by and large I think they did quite a lot of good.

They were extremely well served secretarially, by F. M. Wilkinson who died a year or two ago. You've probably heard of him. And he was a man who was so meticulous everything had to be 110% correct. He became a bottle-neck in the end because everything had to go through him, but nevertheless he was the man who produced the Institute's first Manual, and there was no rival in the field in those days. I think those 'Recommendations' [on Accounting Principles] presented a remarkable step forward. In particular, the later ones on stock were very important because, quite frankly, stock had been pretty slipshod, both in the verification of it and in the valuation of it. As I'm afraid probably even happens still today. There are very large numbers of people who have known Old Joe all his life, and 'he knows what he is doing; and, after all, if it was not showing [in the accounts] this year, it will be in next year: and he gave me these figures on the backs of envelopes and I told him to go back and have them really decently typed out in case I was ever challenged on them - but we can trust Old Joe, and after all he is only doing it for tax, and if he is not paying it this year, he will be paying it next year …'. That was the attitude; it was pretty prevalent.

There was Recommendation N9 on Stocks, I think it was in 1945.

N9. That is right. The [Inland] Revenue got extremely peeved about the slipshod manner in which stocks were taken. They became aware of it, and there was very little they could do. They would ask all sorts of questions, but you know even today, at the end of the day, the man who is responsible knows the answers and no outsider has a chance. You got a series of cases. McKesson versus Robbins in America, where the vats were filled with water instead of hydrochloric acid. You got Cock, Russell & Co. over here, which was 'first in, first out', I think - or Cock, Russell was a 'base stock basis'. There were a whole lot of them. Antofagasta [Railways] - all these cases were symptomatic of the Revenue's frustration, knowing that stock figures were pretty wildly out and they could not possibly get a man to court. So they got him to court on 'first in, first out' or 'base stock' or something like that, you see. That is the way they went about it.

So the Revenue got more and more cross, and about 1953 or 1954 (you could check the dates because it was the year in which Mr Charles Peat, of Peat Marwick, was the President) we had a leak that the Revenue were preparing a new offensive in which they were going to seek powers for Inspectors of Taxes to visit factories and offices and warehouses, and to participate in stock taking. Now that would have been horrible, not so much because of what they would have found - and no doubt they would have found a great deal - but because it would have meant that from that moment onwards the auditor was no longer independent 'in between', looking for the truth, but that he was an agent for the company trying to resist and repel invaders from the Revenue. It was at the Institute's Brighton Conference, I remember very well, that Charles Peat, with his tongue stuck deeply into his cheek, let loose the leak that nobody had heard of before and shocked the profession to its very core: the idea of the Inspector of Taxes walking in and just taking stock. He did it quite deliberately. It caused a great sensation, and it paved the way for the acceptance by members of - what did you say? [Recommendation] N9. I take your word for it - on stock taking.

It might have even been the Institute's taxation conference, but it was in his year [as President]. And I think you'll find that N9 followed within a couple of years of that. You have got to remember all the time that at the Institute we have a constitution that calls for a two-thirds vote, and you will always have a vast number of backwoodsmen who are prepared to vote down 'The Establishment'. And a two-thirds vote on any controversial issue, such as this issue that is coming up now on ethics - whether you can retain a trusteeship in a client company - can have very little chance of success if you get the backwoodsmen coming up to London and throwing their votes in. You have to think in terms of practicabilities. It is all very well for your Director of Studies [i.e. Professor Edward Stamp, then Director of the International Centre for Research in Accounting (ICRA) at Lancaster University, and a vocal critic of the English Institute in the 1970s] to say the Institute hasn't had an idea for years. We are living in the practical world. The whole time it was a matter of making friends and influencing people.

Five votes are important. This is what is often forgotten. People say 'why don't you do this, or why don't you so that?', but it is all within the realms of practical politics. That is why the great inflation debate collapsed - simply because the backwoodsmen got up and said 'too fast, too far, too soon!' [in respect of the Exposure Draft 18 on current cost accounting].

However, let's go back. These people on the Taxation and Financial Research (sic) Committee were working most devotedly in 1941-46 - they produced their Recommendations, which, as I say, were mostly very good. We will come back to the inflation one in a few minutes. Then I think, from about 1946 onwards, they began to sit on their laurels. Am I not right that the Companies Act was in 1947, and it was consolidated in 1948?

That is right.

Now all through 1945-1947 we were debating the Companies Bill, and there is no doubt that an enormous part of the Companies Bill, particularly the Eighth Schedule (on accounting disclosures) stemmed from the work of these T&FR (Taxation and Financial Relations) committees during the war - all their recommendations. That all became law in 1947, consolidated in 1948, and from that time onwards I was conscious that the top people had nailed their flags to the mast and stood by their flags. There was a certain degree of inflexibility. Now if I can illustrate that it is in the inflation debate.

We were all aware in 1945 that the lack of stability in the value of the pound was playing Old Harry with accounts, particularly with the basis of stock valuation and depreciation. We didn't worry much about the finer points, but those were quite clear. We knew that to do anything about it would be extremely complicated, to do the job properly. We took comfort from the fact that the same thing had happened in 1918-1922. My father often told me that he paid £7 for a suit before the First World War, that he paid £22 for it in 1921, and that he got a suit again for £10 in 1922. We felt that if we only bided our time a bit the problem of inflation accounting would go away. We said it was simply not worth the upheaval for 2, 3 or 4%; and in those days it was about 5 or 6% - it wasn't too bad. And so people did not pay a great deal of attention to it, particularly the hierarchy. The Establishment was not very greatly concerned with introducing inflation accounting on any kind of mandatory basis.

Pretty strong representations were however made to the Revenue, because although financial accounts might not take account of it, taxation accounts ought to. And already, before 1945 I think, the established basis of depreciation had been found to be pretty skimpy. And the Chancellor - I forget which one it was - introduced a provision for wear and tear which gave rise to an enormous amount of mirth. He said the wear and tear allowance for tax purposes should be five-fourths 'of what is just and reasonable'. However, when the Second World War came, they toddled along to Stafford Cripps [Chancellor of the Exchequer], who of course was able to grasp the position immediately - his was a brilliant mind. And he saw that if they continued to get depreciation on pre-war values of assets, then the replacement fund would only buy 'half a wheelbarrow' - that is what we used to say.

There was a lot of talk about this in the Budget speeches in 1947 and 1948.

That is right, about that time, and I think even earlier. Wasn't it in 1945 that he introduced 'Initial' and 'Investment' allowances? No, it must have been 1946. The deputations went to see him, and Stafford Cripps said: 'Yes, I understand this, but you can't really expect me, as a poor layman, to charge tax on anything other than what you expert accountants say is the profit. So the sooner you get down to the job I shall be only too happy. But since you tell me it will take a year or more, I will give you temporary relief'. And he invented what is called the 'Initial' and the 'Annual' allowance, which I believe is called these days the 'Investment' allowance.

That was another very big breach because it is an absolute nonsense that you can have 100% depreciation [as a tax allowable expense in the year of purchase]. It was an expedient, not a right; Edmund Burke would have got very angry. It is a concession to expediency rather than to any right principles. But that is how we got the Investment Allowances, which gradually broadened out until we are now [at] 100%. No doubt quite soon we will be given 150% of any money we spend on investment, and then we can all retire.

So that brings us up to the end of the war. And when the war ended, De Paula got up in Council - I wasn't on the Council in those days - [FRM] De Paula got up in Council and said: 'We have got many hundreds, if not thousands, of young men coming back from the Forces. They have been away for five years and we have had Exchange Controls, we have had the Munitions Levy, we have had Excess Profits Tax at 100%, and have had thousands of other things that they've never heard of. The best thing we can do is to give them a welcome home, by way of a refresher course'. So a book was produced, at very short notice, of about 100 pages encapsulating all the things that had happened during the war. And a series of refresher courses were organised up and down the country by the Institute.

And that was my first introduction to the Institute life; as with many other people, all the things I've done have been done by accident - 'because Everest was there'! The senior partner came in one morning and said, 'Kenneth, I have had this letter from Alan McIver, the Secretary of the Institute, saying that they are going to organise some refresher courses, and they want one of our people to go along and talk to them about tax'. And I said 'well, I have never given a talk or lecture at any time in my life'. And he said 'no, but you have been doing Excess Profits Tax for the last five years while these people have been fighting to save us for freedom and democracy, and you are to get down and do it'.

So I mugged it all up, and I learnt far more about Excess Profits Tax than I knew before, and I went down to Downing College, Cambridge, where - I still remember - I was on the left hand side of the quad when this tall, dignified man came towards me and stuck out his hand. And he said 'how do you do? I'm F. R. M. De Paula' - and it all goes back to that. I was very thrilled. The other speaker that evening was a man called Rowland [Stanley Rowland, who worked for de Paula's firm, *de Paula, Lake and Turner*, and subsequently taught at the London School of Economics for some years]. I only mention that because Rowland and I were both deaf, and we both had enormous hearing aids about the size of that [pointing] television set in those days. And we were moving our hearing aids all around the room while these tough chaps from the barrack rooms, the Bruce Sutherlands and Hugh Nicholsons of this world, were having a great time at our expense; but we all became good friends.

Well, as a result of the success of about twenty or thirty of these courses, lasting four or five days each, in 1948 people said 'we ought to have a regular get-together'. And so the first Summer Course was organised at Oxford, at Christ Church. We went to Christ Church for 22 years in succession. A lot of us have spent more than a whole term in Christ Church! Of the 300 that turned up every year, probably a half would be 'old lags', with still the great tradition of the barrack room, all good friends, a good smoking concert - the sort of smoking concert you never have at Lancaster nowadays - wonderful smoking concerts, really good witty things, you know, very clever. And we roared with laughter the whole time, and yet I think we produced an awful lot of very fundamental ideas about all kinds of things. The whole of that practice administration course, for example - you know those booklets? - started at 3 o'clock in the morning at Oxford.

What happened was that Stanley Kitchen and Hugh Nicholson, who were two of the great rebels, had been out on the tiles. But Hugh Nicholson had been told to behave himself because his senior partner, Donald House, was President of the Institute this year. And I was in a room with Appleyard with about five or six others and we were just talking about something in a desultory way when these two came in, quite sober but very happy, and between about 1 o'clock and 4 o'clock they told us all the advanced thinking they had had - annuities for retired partners, borrowed money capital, the form of the partnership deed, the proper age of introducing young partners, how to pay out old partners, specialisation - that was all put down into those practice administration booklets. That was the sort of thing that started.

Then there was a wonderful night we had with Gordon Hunter of Leeds, who is a magistrate, in the chair. And we ran a mock trial of somebody who had not taken a physical stock-taking. I remember that because one of the witnesses who was a Cooper's man who was very keen on physical stock-taking; and the prosecuting counsel knew that they had had a job in Saudi Arabia, and before he knew where he was he had to admit that he hadn't done a physical stock-taking of the harem [laugh]. A good joke - but it pinpointed the thing.

So that was from 1946 onwards. A group of us became friends, and one thing led to another and we all got on each other's committees - we got onto our local district societies. We got onto them not because of ambition, but because we were known and they would nominate you, and things like that, you see. And so when we came back to London at the end of 1948 somebody said: 'Well, we shouldn't just leave this for once a year: let us meet monthly'.

And that was how The 1949 Group started. 25 of us came together, and we are still going strong. I am not an active member now, but I should think we have had, oh, 200-300 meetings. We used to have a meeting at the pub and have some sandwiches and beer and talk for 2½ hours. We would have two 'quickies', lasting a quarter of an hour each, and the recurring theme the whole time in those early years was inflation accounting. We called it replacement cost accounting. And I remember, for example, we were incredibly incensed when we got sight of the Institute's evidence to the Royal Commission on Taxation in 1954, in which they said, as far as I can remember the words, 'there is no great call for members of this profession for any change in the present basis of historic [cost] accounting'.

We were particularly incensed about this because even that year we had had at Christ Church - again, I remember it very well ... I was there when everybody else was out - I arrived, and an old man came into the Common Room and put out his hand. It was the American who set up the first International Congress [of Accounting] in St Louis in 1905 - a Price Waterhouse man, George O. May. And there I was with this wonderful old man - he was about 80 then. He had been talking inflation accounting for 20-odd years. We all took it up in The 1949 Group, in the Summer Courses, and we put in representations to the Royal Commission on Taxation to the effect that the evidence given to them by the official Council of the Institute did not represent the views of many of its members. Thomas Robson was absolutely furious. So we were very concerned with it from the very word go. I must not go on forever; I'm boring you.

Well, no! This I find extraordinarily interesting, because you find that at this time, both with the Millard Tucker Committee and then with the Royal Commission on Taxation, you had not just the Society of Incorporated Accountants and Auditors, and the Association of Certified and Corporate Accountants and the Institute of Cost and Works Accountants, as they then were, all in favour of replacement cost accounting, but you also have a very significant group within the Institute!

Oh, undoubtedly. I mean, I was talking about this, stomping the country about it. I remember I commented favourably on it in *The Economist*. I used to write for *The Economist* for 20-odd years. In 1951, I think, there was something about it being high time it came. And this has been the biggest tragedy of my professional life: it is so unutterably, irrefutably right that there should be some form of inflation accounting. I learnt it in many ways. I learnt it as an articled clerk. I was an economics graduate, but I was only a second year articled clerk when I suddenly realised that because of inflation in China, the devaluation of the Yen or whatever the currency was, it only took the profit of one hour's working of this Chinese company to write off the whole of its fixed assets. So I realised there was something wrong.

And then I did the audit of a very well known firm of coin dealers in London, and I found that they had put all their pre-war stock into bank vaults, because they were not going to sell their pre-war stock at inflated prices and pay Excess Profits Tax on it. During the war, they made their living by going out and buying in the morning and selling in the afternoon, and making their 10%. They weren't going to sell a £1 coin for a £100 and pay £99 tax!

The best story, I'm sure you know it, is about the German hardware merchant in 1922 in Dusseldorf who was very careful and prepared monthly accounts. He had ten bags of nails, and he sold them and made a profit; and he was very cautious about it and ploughed back half of his profits. Well, there was 25% accelerating inflation per month at that time, and after 12 months of doing this he, being a very cautious man, found he had only 1 nail left. So he changed his policy. He drove the nail into the wall and hanged himself. [laugh] I mean, that is a perfectly possible story of what happens if you get into inflation.

It is so evident. If you do your fixed assets on that basis, you end up at the end of the day with enough money to buy 'half a wheelbarrow'; and you can't run a factory on half a wheelbarrow! This discussion has been going on for a long time. Ted Parker [W. E. - later Sir Edmund - Parker] did a lot of work on it. When inflation was only 6 or 7%, people would never really get down to it and so we weren't prepared for the inflation when it came after the Arab-Israel War in 1974.

The peak I think had been something like 11% in 1947.

Had it been as high as that?

I think so, yes.

I think part of the blame, you know, is that the one thing that will make accountants and their clients (and the clients are more important really than the accountants!) really face up to it is the tax situation. The tax people have always made the mistake of giving us what we ask for without our altering the accounts. If we only got historic depreciation, we would not hear from all these people who are shouting about the Institute passing it up - the Midlands group of industrial accountants; the '100 Group' of industrial accountants; and 101 university professors of one kind or another. You are all snarling at the Institute for not doing something about it - but the trouble is that whenever we try to do anything, vested interest always stands in the way.

The business man knows best - he does not want to be told by any bookkeeper what his profits are: 'Look here, man, I'm the chap who runs this show. I am responsible: I know!' Secondly, the business man absolutely loves: 'I am glad to tell you that once again our turnover was a record for the fifth year running, and our profits are 3% higher than the previous year, and now a vote of thanks all round...'. The trade unions will have nothing to do with it. They want to say: 'Well, Fords have made £350 million of profit, and it is no good their telling us they want to knock off £200 million for special depreciation - that is a capitalist dodge!'. The economists don't really want it because they say that there is something subjective about inflation accounting. The government don't want it because they haven't thought of it themselves. I mean, the way they behaved about supporting Sandilands was perfectly disgraceful. You saw them at lunch today - they were all round you [at the Reform Club]. The chap behind you was John Green, Deputy Chairman of the Board of Inland Revenue. They're the 'Mandarins' - they know best. We are the 'naughty children who should do what Whitehall tell you!' [laugh] So there is a very big vested interest against any particular change.

Going back to Sandilands, we produced current cost accounting - I suppose you could almost call that 'index linking', can't you? I am out of touch with the technicalities of it now; I know that I thought it was getting a bit sophisticated at some of its edges. But, basically, it was a great deal better than nothing. If you sold £100 this year and £200 next year, under the historical basis you could say 'my sales have gone up by a 100%'. If the price level has doubled, however, under current purchasing power you say you were just level pegging. It was simple as that, without any fuss and bother. People put whiskers on all this simplicity - I said 'pity my simplicity' - and they have made it intensely complicated. I don't think current purchasing power was too bad. I thought it got 90% right; we put enormous educational effort into it. We had people like Peter Clayton [sent by Mr Wright's firm, Dearden Farrow, to take the M.A. in Accounting and Finance at Lancaster in 1973; later a partner in charge of the Warwick office] talking to our clients. We had books published, we had information guides, we had courses and all the rest of it, and it was all ready to go. And I had been in office [as President of the Institute] for about a month.

Well, we had to work with the government, rather than against it. There is the old motto when you come against opposition that 'the best way to beat them is to join them'. So we accepted the Sandilands Report, but took good care that we were the people who were appointed to put it into a blueprint. Now, Douglas Morpeth - for whom I have the highest admiration - he had a very, very rough deal indeed. It is easy to make mock of a situation when it is over, but he was given an impossible task to do, and we did not believe in Sandilands.

But the Institute, if it has a failing, it is that it can't do a job in a general way - it always has to go to town and do it thoroughly. And we know what happened when Morpeth did it thoroughly; it was 400 pages and it scared the pants off everybody! Morpeth could say: 'yes, and if I had not said what would happen to the indexation of debts as well as the indexation of positive assets or leases, I would have been blamed for not doing a proper job'. He did a proper job. But the backwoodsmen said 'not on your Nelly!'. It was a great tragedy, and I think it goes back to what I said at the beginning: we lived in a simple, simplistic world - it wasn't a bad one at all. The world was going to become a lot more complicated because of all the new taxes and so forth, but I also think that an awful lot of people are to blame.

We are too controversial a profession; anything that is put up by the accountants will be torn to shreds and pieces, and a hundred and ten alternative decisions put in. You academics have got quite a share of the blame; I think industry has an enormous part of the blame; and I think our own members and our own firms. I know that *Accountancy Age* is only there to whip up dissension between one firm and another, but it does seem to me, looking through it, that as soon as the Institute says something, someone else has to get publicity by putting the contrary view somewhere, out of self-respect not to agree. It was Coleridge who said that the great art is the willing suspension of disbelief. I wish some of my colleagues would heed that. I think they go in too much for the minutiae of the whole thing, and lose sight of the great design.

To defend academics in general from the charge that we are inclined to look for faults instead of looking for merit, I think in the past, until fairly recently - until the last ten years - one had a sense of shadow-boxing. It was very hard indeed to know where the ideas were coming from. Things were not done in public very often, as you said earlier on. Things tended to be discussed first and then a view expressed.

But surely we are now exposing all those drafts in a tremendous way, and the point of exposing them is that people address their minds to it, they come to a dozen different conclusions, those conclusions are all considered, and each person by the very effort of considering it has convinced himself that he is right. The Institute chooses one out of the twelve, and so it has eleven dissatisfied customers on every occasion.

I'm not at all convinced that the dissatisfactions are nearly as serious a matter under these circumstances as they were before.

Yes, but you see our problem don't you?

Oh yes, absolutely. I am involved in the Accounting Standards Technical Committee at the Association of Certified Accountants, and we have discussed this new draft on current cost accounting. And people have said 'well, I'm not happy about this bit or that bit' and we have had the thing thrashed out in the open. And we were prepared to say at the end of the day that we think this is a pretty good proposal and we are going to give it our whole-hearted backing. I think this has come at the end of a very full debate in which a lot of different views have been expressed, and I think it has been a fairly productive effort.

Well, of course, you can't expect one man to hit the right bulls-eye, but when you have half a dozen views you get into compromises. And when you have six different Institutes you multiply that still further.

The difficulty with compromises is that you end up with internal contradictions, principles that are totally at odds with one another in the same document. I think the first draft we saw from Hyde had this sort of problem. It was not clearly measuring the profits of the entity or of the shareholders - it was a mixture of the two. Once they are pulled apart, then the whole thing makes a lot of sense.

Could I go back to the 1940s for a minute, to the question of the sources of ideas. I get the impression from talking to one or two people who were involved the debate at that time that the ideas were being evolved, discussed, thrashed out at Oxford and so on. But there was not very much continuity with the earlier American academic writing on the subject - a book by Henry Sweeney, for example, in 1936 called *Stabilized Accounting*.

We nearly always had one overseas speaker at Oxford. I think it was very much more practical than comparable courses would be today. Have you ever seen the papers that were written at Oxford?

Not at Oxford, no.

There were three papers to each conference, and they would be on stock, or in my case on partnership goodwill, and retirement annuities and things like that. Very practical papers. I don't think we went into a great deal of theory: a lot of Eighth Schedule stuff and so forth. How the ideas occurred, I don't know.

You mentioned, for example, Gilbert Garnsey's influence. Garnsey would probably have been aware of the stuff which had been written in America, by British people mainly -

[Arthur Lowes] Dickinson, yes -

- on the origins of consolidations, going back to 1900. The Americans, with their environment, needed consolidations very badly, with lots of different States and lots of companies formed in those States. They badly needed the idea, where it wasn't necessary over here in Britain. And there were intellectual reservations in this country over consolidation anyway because there was no such thing as a group of companies in law, and people were very upset about that idea. In that area there are some fairly clear pointers as to why ideas developed as they did. In the area of inflation accounting it is not quite so clear. It is not so clear whether people were concerned by tax, whether for capital maintenance and reinvestment, whether they were concerned because they were adding unlike monetary units - 1939 pounds to 1949 pounds -and so on.

Yes - chalk and cheese.

I think the answer is probably a mix of these.

I think it was purely pragmatic. In my case, as I say, I was convinced (a) because of the Chinese Mining Company, and (b) because of the coin dealer who wouldn't sell old stock, (c) because of the hardware merchant in Dusseldorf, and because of the 'half wheelbarrow'. I don't think you need to be interested in theory - it is just obvious! [laugh].

What about the Price Commission? There were price controls in the 1940s.

In the war?

In the wartime, yes.

Oh yes. I didn't have a great deal to do with this. I just had to do one small thing, in copper. But I did not get into that field at all. Anything that I did in the practical way was on the taxation side.

The other important development during the 1940s was in cost accounting.

Yes, you are onto the wrong man there. I am absolutely no good at management or cost accounting at all. I can only talk nonsense about it!

Just to go back to one little side line on the tax side, I believe the 1940s and the early 1950s was a period when the Institute really made tremendous progress with taxation and had a great deal to be rather proud of. You see, we had this great big Colossus of a man, Sir William Carrington, who was the biggest tax man in the country and a tremendous character, for whom I have a great admiration. He was on the Royal Commission [on Taxation], and he was on both Millard Tucker Committees. We at the Institute were activated by his enthusiasm in a way; we worked and worked and worked, and we put in a whole year's recommendations to the 1954 Royal Commission and to Millard Tucker. We policed them fairly carefully afterwards. They were very well received. About 1963/64 I used to keep a list of the things that came out in the Finance Bill, and you could always tick off our recommendations as having been introduced. It was generally recognised that we had the finest system of loss relief in the world; and a particular problem was retirement benefits for the self employed, where up to 1956 the self-employed could only provide for their retirement out of net income and the disadvantages were tremendous. We worked very hard on that for six or seven years.

Now by 'we' at this stage, who do you mean exactly?

The Taxation Sub-Committee of the Institute, bubbling over onto the Oxford Summer School, bubbling over onto The 1949 Group. I remember when R.A. Butler went off to Australia with the report of the second Millard Tucker Committee in his briefcase and our evidence. He came back a week before the budget without having read it - and he did nothing.

We burst forth then, and the following year we mounted a very big campaign. We wrote 4,000 - 5,000 letters; we got the public analysts, we got the veterinary surgeons, we got the barristers, the lawyers, the doctors, the whole medical profession; we all bombarded our MPs with letters. We had letters in *The Times, The Financial Times, The Lancet, The Investor's Chronicle, The Economist* and so forth. We went in deputations to meet the Labour people at the House of Commons, and to meet the Conservatives at the House of Commons. That was a very big exercise in public relations. Macmillan was the chancellor in 1956, and when he sat down [after the Budget speech] he turned to his neighbour and said, 'well I hope those chartered accountants in the City are satisfied now!'. [laugh]

It has made a world of difference, you see. There were two worlds before. I mean, you on your pension fund - the university provides 8%, you provide your 8% or whatever the rates are nowadays - we were really getting very low about that time. And that was a pace-maker. Actually, when it came out I wrote 4,000 words for *The Economist* in one day on it, and I am told that my article in *The Economist* was read out at Congress, and it has gone in the Congress Library because they were years behind us in getting self employed relief.

So on taxation we did frightfully well. Then came 1965 and - well, I must be very careful; it made practically everything I had known and believed in obsolete. I had no great joy in Corporation Tax as a separate thing, because I think it is misconceived in principle. And although I think there is a very sound case indeed for Capital Gains Tax, there are a lot of 'ifs' and 'buts' about the Capital Gains Tax, you see. It was all different.

You're asking me what happened between 1935 and 1955. It was a period of very considerable tax reform. We did an enormous amount of work on things like the erosion of the tax base. I'm very much a 'Kaldorite'.

You believe in an Expenditure Tax?

Yes, but you could not say so openly otherwise you'd have been shot at dawn. Well, I've said enough, I think.

Well, there are one or two lines that I'd still like to ask about, if I may. For example, the effects of the merger with the Society [of Incorporated Accountants and Auditors]. How did they join in? Did they come in on a whole-hearted basis in 1957? Were they welcomed?

I can't speak off the back of my head about the development of the two sides. I did read the other day that the Institute is producing something for the Centenary [a history of the Institute was published in 1965]. Of course, the Society was led in the most dynamic way by a man called Martin. The Society and the Institute were much closer to one another than the Association because there was a very substantial practising side to the Society. About 25 years ago two men crossed over to America together on the same boat to attend the American conference; one was Donald House, of the Institute, and the other was Bertram Nelson from the Society. And they just sat, and Bertram Nelson in the lovely throw-away way that he has (which you could hardly ever hear - that is the great trouble with Bertram: it is so hard to hear what he says) suggested that they should come together. And they decided it was a good idea, and came back and did it.

That had to be very, very carefully orchestrated. Sir William Lawson was a very big man in it. He stumped the country and so forth. Sir Henry Benson I think was very much in favour of it. And it was touch and go - '66%' came into it (the need for a two-thirds majority vote in favour of a change).

Incidentally, just as an amusing side-line, my firm were the scrutineers in that election. We used to go along every day to the Institute, three of us - it was quite exciting, because at an Institute election in the first few days if you are pro-Institute your heart rises, and you get 70 or 80% 'yes'. All the 'good boys' just tick it off, and put it in the post and don't think any more about it. So you get 70% or more for the first three or four days, and then you get a bad week and all the 'nos' are mustered. As a matter of fact, a vast number of replies came back without a stamp on, and we thought we would do a little exercise. We thought it would be all the 'naughty boys' saying 'no' who would send their replies back without a stamp on. The lack of stamping was exactly equal between the yes's and the no's! [laugh].

Anyway, by the end of the second week it was down to about 65% 'yes' replied overall. Gloom! And then came the overseas votes. And the overseas came in 'yes', 'yes', 'yes', 'yes'…during the third and fourth weeks. The overseas members would not be affected by the dilution to the same extent. They would only pay a minor subscription. If you want to get away with things - with a subscription increase - you make a composite resolution, and make sure quite a substantial minority are given benefits (like the Welsh miners are going to be given tomorrow afternoon), and they'll all vote 'yes' and the people whose subscriptions go up from £50 to £2,000 won't have a say. A cynical way of doing it [laugh]; but there is a lot of politics in all this.

It was very carefully orchestrated. It was 1958. I was London chairman at the time, and we were very, very carefully briefed. I remember the meeting at which I introduced it to the committee of the London District Society. I'd really done my homework, and I gave an exposition and then asked for questions. Somebody asked me about section 15(b), which was a tricky one. The whole of section 15 was pretty tricky, and I had mastered it. I gave them an exposition which left them spell bound - their mouths dropped open. Three months later, somebody said to me: 'You realise that when you were asked that question and you gave that brilliant exposition of section 15(b), you were asked what section 15(d) meant!' [laugh].

Another little side-line on that. In the first elections to the London District Society after the merger, there were six vacancies and there were seven candidates for them. Six of the candidates were chartered accountants, one was an ex-Society man. There was no doubt at all in my mind that if it went to the election, the chartered people would get in and the Society man would be left out - not out of beastliness, but simply because they were better known. And I thought that if that happened - and the President, who was Sir William Lawson, worked with me on this - if the Society had their man thrown out at the first election, it would make a rift that would never be healed. So I went out of my way, and I went to the most likeable of the six chartered accountant members and asked him to wait until next year, which he did willingly. So there was an unopposed election.

Those little bits of care are exercised in the Institute all the way down the line. It is very good diplomacy. We are still, of course, the six groups in spite of that [the six UK based professional bodies]. The government are always harking on about how they didn't want six different opinions about accountancy - couldn't they have one. And, naturally enough, the English Institute is the unpopular body, because 'big brother' is always unpopular. Ontario is unpopular in Canada, New York is unpopular in America, New South Wales is unpopular in Australia, the Transvaal is unpopular in South Africa - so England is unpopular in accounting in the United Kingdom.

On the other hand, Big Brother does carry a very large part of the burden, if not the money. We had certainly put in, I think, more physical effort into the Recommendations and things like that than had the other bodies, and, above all, being in London we were very much at the centre of things. I mean, Whitehall turned to us. Very naturally, the other bodies tended to get a chip on the shoulder if the English Institute told the Department of Trade this, that or the other. It was Lord Lewisham who said: 'You people really ought to get together, somehow or other'. Well, we knew perfectly well that union had already failed [in the integration debate of 1969/1970], hadn't it? We were the snobs. And there again you've got the 'two thirds', and you've got the country practitioner who doesn't want somebody he regards as having had a lesser training - who has not been through Articles or something like that. It is the old demarcation problem that you have got in every trades union in the country.

And so in 1971/72 the first talks were about joining the six bodies together into the CCAB. Douglas Morpeth and Alec Mackenzie of Scotland - they were the two leaders of it; I tagged along as a deputy at that time. And then the next year it came to fruition. We had quite a lot of hard work. I pay a very, very great tribute to Bill Crawford, the Scottish secretary. He died very suddenly a couple of months ago, down here at Greenwich. We saw a lot of him and his wife. He suddenly had a heart attack, I think, at dinner at the Royal Naval College. He was a diplomat all the way through.

There was a tremendous amount of giving and taking on both sides. I was being forced into a corner as the leader of the unpopular Big Brother, and I had to decide when I could give way and so forth because I had right-wingers behind me - I had to guard my own rear. And I remember Bill Crawford at the end, in my bedroom in Stockholm at the fiftieth anniversary of the Swedish Institute. We all got together at 10.30 in the morning over some coffee - unmade beds - and there was one final problem to be overcome. We had to meet the ladies at 12.15. At 12 o'clock, Bill Crawford said: 'Well, you know Kenneth's given away an awful lot. He has got some very wild men all round him. We have got to meet the ladies. I think we can agree on this, don't you?' [laugh]. By which time Alan Nelson for the Association could say 'I suppose so'. It was not a matter of any fundamental problem by this time.

Yes. It does seem to have been quite a success, the CCAB.

Yes, I think there is a good deal of criticism of the scale of things and the expense. Everybody was in favour of all being one, all the representations going in under a joint name: there was not quite so much enthusiasm when we have to pay for it!

Just a final word; I'd like to question if we are not getting a bit over-complicated. Granted, we were too simple altogether fifty years ago. It seems to me - I don't want to be unfair at all; it is terrible of old men to say 'I wouldn't have done it this way' - but it does seem to be getting a bit too complex. Too many voices, too much babble, too much being published. I think we are being over-governed. We are telling our members what to do. We have got manuals, we have got guides, we have got disciplinary committees and so forth, and it is absolutely in the trend. The whole profession is a bureaucracy. People are organising, fixing insurance policies for negligence, all sorts of things like those. It is symptomatic of the whole country. We are all doing financial sector stuff; there is hardly anybody on a machine, making a lathe go round.

But, there again I welcome the increasing participation of the academics - but you've got to find a single voice, just like CCAB has had to find a single voice. We can't go on offending the 99% of you because we can only choose one solution out of a 100. I mean, I don't know Lawson at all well [Gerry Lawson, Professor of Finance at Manchester Business School] but I imagine he doesn't think very highly of us because we haven't absorbed his problems of cash flow in place of depreciation.

Well, I hope you would not be surprised to hear it, but I would agree with you absolutely on that. I tend to think that this is a fault which we exhibit in all sorts of areas of life.

My son has just left this country for America, for a small outfit in America where they do things. They built a new factory since last November, these people.

I also have a misgiving in the back of my mind over the number of accountants on the boards of companies, rather than engineers.

Yes, that is right. Our son was doing terribly well, he was being very, very well treated by his company. But he is an engineer and he said his company was very arts-orientated not engineering-orientated. There is a sort of Parkinson's law you know. I've seen this in the Institute's committees. You get into a troublesome area and, before you know where you are, if you go out of the room in the Institute when you come back you find you've been put on three new committees [laugh].

And, of course, there is a lack of the really powerful man. The powerful man has disappeared, hasn't he, since Carlyle and Winston Churchill and Henry Benson and one or two others. There is nobody a hero any more.

Well, I think the man who is effective is the man who is powerful in that he is clear and knows precisely what it is that he is advocating, having sounded out views and having considered the views expressed to him. This is the great art. We had a pretty effective Vice-Chancellor at

Lancaster. Charles Carter was like that. He would listen to the views, but at the end of the day he knew where he stood.

He would make up his own mind. He is a Quaker, too.

Who were the people in The 1949 Group who got it under way? Yourself?

Oh yes. Peter Morgan-Jones of Eastbourne - he is with 'The Thundering Herd', Thornton Baker. There was Hugh Nicholson of course.

You met in London?

Yes, we were a London group. The 'Deloitte' President of the Institute - Guy Densem. David Cawson of Coopers; James Mann, of Mann Judd. Then a single practitioner called Armitage, of Enfield. There were about twenty-five of us, and I suppose on average about three or four dropped out every year, and three or four new ones came in.

You would decide at one meeting what you were going to talk about at the next?

That is right, yes. In the very early days of Lord Wolfson we had a lovely debate: 'Thank God for the take-over bid'. It was really shaking up British boardrooms, you see. I know we went in very great detail into a scheme to take over Turner & Newall. (If you were interested, I could tell you about it - no, I don't think I could. I think I've just destroyed all my files.) As I said, they have had about 170 meetings. We would always have one meeting on Budget day every year.

And did someone give a paper?

A paper, yes. A 25-minute paper, with half an hour's discussion, half an hour for the 'quickies', and half an hour for the sandwiches. Let me see. Douglas Morpeth was a member; Guy Densem was a member; I was a member. We were all given a piece of silver - the three of us became Presidents [of the Institute]. I think nearly everybody else was on committees. Godfrey Judd was on the Council; James Mann was on the Council; Bill Fea - he was British Steel Corporation - he was on the Council.

These were lunch-time meetings or evening meetings?

Evening. People could not come at lunch, so 6.30pm-9.00pm, something like that.

It sounds a very useful group. It sounds as though it performed a rather similar role to the London District Society, but much more concentrated.

We were quite unofficial. The Council used to get very cross with us. I remember somebody said 'who is this 1949 Group?'. I said 'well, it is the group which produced Guy Densem, Douglas Morpeth and Godfrey Judd, and James Mann and Hugh Nicholson and Brian Maynard' - not Brian Maynard; he wasn't a member Brian Sutherland. You ought to see Brian Sutherland, you know. He is a bright fellow. He is a sole practitioner who lives in a manor house in Morton-in-the-Marsh or somewhere like that. He has got a very bright brain, has Bruce.

He and Hugh Nicholson were the two people who killed integration. They were very, very highly skilled. I was on the inside and they were on the outside, and anything that we did at the Institute had to be careful, it had to exact, precise, comprehensive, dignified and so forth. It meant the Institute's image. We couldn't lose our tempers; we couldn't say rash things; we couldn't appeal to the emotions. And they for their part were a highly skilled couple and felt very seriously about it. It wasn't just a rag for them. They produced some brilliant literature: just one page - and the number of things they didn't put into that paper was tremendous! But they just got the bull's-eye, you see.

It is like fighting guerrillas; the guerrillas always win in the short run. I could go out into Pall Mall and shoot half a dozen people; nobody would stop me. They'd get me in the end, but to begin with I'd win. And that is what they did.

What about relations with the universities? Was there much connection before the war?

Not much. One of the key figures was Bertram Nelson. He knows more Vice-Chancellors than I know fellow chartered accountants. We had a feeling that we had muddy boots; certainly, very few people were graduates. The thing to do was to get the trial balance to balance. Gradually the feeling grew that we ought to have greater respectability.

Now P.D. Leake, who was before my time, was one of the early thinking accountants. He wrote a lot about goodwill. When he died, about 1943, he left his money not to the Institute itself but to a Trust to be administered by the Institute, for the advancement of the profession of accounting and public finance. He died in 1943 and his estate consisted largely of rubber estates in Sumatra, under the occupation of the Japanese, and of shares in the Ritz Hotel, Paris, occupied by the Germans. The estate duty problems were negligible. So nothing happened until after the war. The Japanese left Sumatra, the Germans left the Ritz Hotel, and when the estate was sold up there was about £300,000 of money with no estate duty on it. So the question was what to do with it, and we thought we would go round searching for respectability.

We went to Oxford and were told that they didn't do such things. Then we went to Cambridge, where they were very, very cautious indeed. And in the end they said they could only do it on certain terms, which was, as you well know, a life chair and so forth. But beggars couldn't be choosers. We accepted their terms, which gave us the minimum of say or control over what the chap could do. And it was put out to advertisement.

I was extremely interested because I had been twenty-odd years in the profession, and I had about twenty years to go, and I was interested in the issues and writing every week in *The Economist*, and I was getting lectures all over the country, and I am a Cambridge economics graduate. So I thought about high table and being a member of a college and things like that. I spent a lot of time on it, actually. One of my partners took me aside and said I was under a contract with him for seven years; I could break it unilaterally, but he would be sorry to see me go because it would upset the balance of the firm.

I was quite serious and then I got cold feet because a research fellow cannot have a college office, and I wouldn't have minded if I would have been financial bursar, and dealt with the college's investments and got on the telephone to talk to the stockbroker and that sort of thing. I wouldn't have minded if I could be teaching; but I thought that to be a research fellow - to get up at 9 o'clock on a Monday morning, and go into my study and start to read about inflation in Brazil - it was a terrible way to spend the rest of my life. And I pulled out of it.

I never applied, but I was very interested. And it was due to be announced on a certain day, and it didn't come out. I thought this was funny, and I rang up the editor of *The Times* Educational Supplement and he said: 'it should have come out yesterday, Mr Wright, but something's up. I'll let you know'. And he came back and said 'well I don't know what it is, but they have taken it back, and now they've brought up Stone'.

What they were really doing was that they wanted our £3,000 really to finance something that J.R.N. Stone was already doing. He was a very nice chap, I know. Bertram [Nelson] was the liaison man with him. I spent the night up at Cambridge with them. To see Stone sprawling over his table with his work was quite fascinating. Far better than reading it. It is unreadable. But I reckon we got poor value out of that £3,000 a year!

Well, it has not done much for the accounting profession; it has been jolly useful research to have done. And certainly Stone is very important in national income measurement.

It is not our idea of income. That was the background of that.

He must have been the initiative behind the joint Working Party, which was set up by the Institute with the National Institute of Economics Social Research (NIESR).

I don't know anything about that.

I think I've got the paper here. Yes I have, I have got it here. This was the Joint Exploratory Committee, who published in 1951. Joint Exploratory Committee appointed by the English Institute and the NIESR and the people who were involved ......

- this is right in the middle of my time.

It is a very, very interesting piece of work. [Reading] Who was Henry Clay?

[Reading] Oh, Harry Norris, yes; and P. M. Rees; Lawrence Robson; Basil Smallpeice; and Turner. Clay? I think he was a civil servant.

He was appointed by the NIESR.

[Reading] Geoffrey Crowther, the economist. I'd forgotten about him until seeing his name.

The Report was set up in 1946 and came out in 1951.

Oh - 1951? That is before my time, largely.

They were looking for common definitions, and they could not really find them. But it is interesting that the initiative was taken at that time.

Harry Norris was a member of The 1949 Group in the very early days. He was the group leader of the first of the Summer courses I went to. Lawrence Robson of course is the Liberal Party leader. We know him and his wife. At the first Autumn conference we went to, at Brighton in 1947, his wife was there. She is now Lady Robson. She really was a glamour piece. She didn't wear anything round her waist which rather fascinated accountants in 1947 [laugh]. [Reading] Reddaway read economics with me at Cambridge.

You were reading economics between 1930 and 1933?

About 1930 to 1932, in the middle of the depression, yes. I had one go under Keynes. I was never in the Keynes club; but it was rather wonderful having sat under him.

Well, we had better be on our way.

I am most grateful to you.

Jack Clayton

Interviewed by

Michael Mumford

24th May 1979 at Lancaster University

We have been talking about the purchasing power of the pound from the 15th century.

This is a chart I did of the pound. [Showing document]

You'd expect there to be greater fluctuations at the time of war. Now, the Black Death would have been deflationary, but you would have expected some of the wars like the '100 Years War' period to have been pretty inflationary, wouldn't you?

Well, it was up and down, but I think by and large what happened was that - this is a very interesting feature - shortly after the Norman Conquest until Henry, the English sterling silver penny from Offa's time onwards was the common currency in the 'Common Market' of Europe, because it had such a stable silver content and it was only Henry who mucked it up. I have on my wall a very precious little document; it is opposite where I do my typing. It is the neatest little act of Elizabeth, saying what she did with the people who mucked about with her currency. She hanged them; she had them hanged, drawn and quartered and the bowels burnt before they were quite dead. And she did her very best to stop the inflation which was started by her father.

So two features are most interesting to me. One was the relative stability during the Middle Ages. By and large it was when the coins became worn and defaced by wear and tear and the actions of the criminals, and the poor Kings had to re-coin them, that they found they hadn't enough silver, and they [the coins] gradually lost half their weight. I think that was the real reason for the devaluation in the Middle Ages. The other interesting feature is here: the gold sovereign of Edward VII bought 50% more than that of his great grandfather, George III. And you see what happened. It is very different from the present devaluation of the pound. That is something I've just had rejected by *The Guardian*. I was hoping they'd publish this. I did something on this some time ago; it was very interesting. I didn't try and publish it myself. I distributed it to some of my friends in the press, and one friend in particular, Tony Harris of the *Financial Times* used it. It was never acknowledged, but it was the basis of one of his middle page articles. When I challenged him - I play bridge with him - he said: 'Of course, I edited it'. But this is it: I've just done it again. This is the most interesting graph. I believe our inflation is mostly home produced and not imported. Not only that, I don't think it is anything to do with high wages - I think it is entirely public spending.

Before going on to that, I find that interesting [pointing to the 16th century on the graph]. You would expect there to be a very strong inflationary pressure on the discovery of the New World, and the capture of Spanish gold and all that business.

Well it wasn't that; it was Henry who did that. It was Henry's deliberate devaluation. It was a great debasement by Henry VIII. He took ¾ of the gold and silver content out of the coinage. Then Queen Elizabeth [1st] and company started very hard to stop it.

And it didn't have an immediate effect?

Well, it was a matter of Gresham's Law - bad money drove out good. And then - my comments are a bit flippant - despite Nell Gwynne and chopping the King's head off, matters were not too bad [during the 17th century].

Yes, over that period it was an extraordinarily stable, wasn't it? The whole of the 17th up to the middle of the 18th century.

Yes. Then the industrial revolution comes, of course.

Well, that could have had either effect couldn't it? There, from the second half of the 18th century there was a time of considerable inflation, and then the Industrial Revolution was increasing the purchasing power of the pound.

It was one of the effects of the Industrial Revolution. This, I think, was our great century of productivity. In the 19th century, you see, we had a twelve-times increase in Gross National Product [GNP] and a four times increase in population, so we had 3½ times productivity; that was the real issue there. I think that is the basic reason, rather than the question of gold discoveries. But since the Second World War, of course, it is all changed. And here is the answer to that.

Yes. Now then - let's have a look at this.

Look at the top ground first; that is a unique approach - I don't think anybody else has tried it. What I've done there is to take public spending relative to the GNP. I've taken out consumer spending which is privately financed - that is, eliminating that part which is public spending, OK?

Certainly, yes.

That is grants and new houses.

Yes, certainly. Housing would be excluded.

This is the 'Wynne Godley' concept that I'm talking about.

Yes, but it would exclude pension rights?

It excludes pensions and excludes debt interest, the two main elements. By the way, as regards growth, something I did a few years ago - I know Jack Hibbert quite well; I've had a lot to do with him. I never met him, but we have had a lot of telephone calls. In 1973, I think 1973/74, when the terms of trade went against us, you had the unique position that at current prices we had an export deficit - we had a deficit on balance of payments - but at constant prices we had a surplus. And so I challenged it and said: 'this is wrong'. We had a hell of a battle and finally I wrote it up, actually in *The Accountant*. He challenged me, and he didn't take my pants off - I took his off! He said I didn't understand the figures - what the base was, but I was able to challenge him, from his own book of definitions, as a result of which he said: 'OK; well, we had better have an article in *Economic Trends*' and we got a group together. I'm not sure whether Wynne Godley was one of them. He got a group of professors writing about this, trying to blind me with science. But the outcome was that the only way they could shut me up was by inventing this completely new index of disposable income, which is better and more reliable I think - I think they themselves admit as much. Well, that is why they invented it - it is a more reliable measure of growth than Gross Domestic Product [GDP]. And that is what I've used.

Yes. GDP is a difficult one anyway, isn't it?

Well, I've used this disposable income measure, particularly as I'm basing it on GNP, and this index does include income from abroad. The interesting thing is that consumers' expenditure has progressed at less than half the rate of the growth of the economy, but public expenditure at more than twice the rate. Now then, see the actual trend pre-war. Pre-war consumers' expenditure was about 75%. The period I've taken - because I've taken great interest in this period, in fact my first essay in economic writing was when I read Reggie Maudling's two million 4% growth plan in 1963 and I said that this was likely to bust the pound. In fact, I gave it an amusing title [reading]. There we are: 'Stop eating the Seed-corn'. This is what I said about the pound.

These arguments are very similar to those I've heard from Lawrence Robson; do you know him?

Lawrence is a very old friend of mine. When I retired, he wanted me to become his senior partner in Leeds.

In Robson Rhodes?

Yes. Oh, Lawrence and I are very old friends. I was largely responsible for Lawrence getting on the Council, because they had black-balled him.

Good gracious.

This is what I said about it [inflation] here. And this is where I started my campaign against the excessive public expenditure. And I've been at it ever since. Now I've got allies.

Yes, I suppose that a simplistic Keynesian start would be to say, if you are going to have a shift of expenditure from the private sector to the public sector, as long as one is reducing consumption in the private

sector by the same amount as the expenditure in the public sector, the net effect ought to be very little indeed.

I don't agree.

But that begs the question whether what you are taking out of the private sector would have a propensity to consume of a 100% anyway; in other words, whether the marginal propensity to consume is as high in the private sector as it is in the public sector.

No: but this is it. I think there is a new factor. Colin Clarke was a man who said: 'There is only room for two theorists in any generation - the rest of us must build brick by brick'. Now this is what I tried to do. Based upon my building up brick by brick, I've developed a theory. I do not think - and you see I've got the evidence - I do not think that you can keep on depressing (as has been done particularly viciously by [Denis] Healey, helped by [Aubrey] Jones) - I don't think you can keep on forcing down the standard of living of the working population to support a higher standard of living for the non-working population than we can afford. Now, I think that is what has happened, and that is what is underlying the tremendous clamour for wages. I've got a feeling in my bones that once you get this consumption below 50%, I think you are in trouble because of the concept of relative wages - the feeling of the producers that they are entitled to a fair whack of what they produce. They want the motor cars, they want the television, they want the things that are produced. And, as Mrs Thatcher and company and her mob saw clearly, they want the houses too. Jim Callaghan played hell with his boys last night; he said: 'look, you are going to put the Tories in for ever? Everybody wants a house and everybody wants those things'.

Yes that is right.

Did you see my latest published thing: 'Less Tax and more Law and Order'?

I have been ploughing a very narrow furrow for the last year or so, and I had a very heavy administrative load here for the first six years. So I've not read widely at all. I've kept my eyes down very much on the stuff that I have to keep ticking over. So I have not.

Have you got back files of *The Accountant* to look at, or shall I give you a copy?

We take *The Accountant* in the library.

Oh well; look at May 3rd [1979], because I didn't go to bed the previous Wednesday night to get it done. I wanted it on Maggie's desk [Margaret Thatcher] and [Geoffrey] Howe's desk the next day. And I took my title, obviously, from Maggie's great speech at the dissolution debate: 'Less Tax and More Law and Order'. I put forward proposals for a complete reform of the taxation system.

On what principles?

Corporation tax first. I fought for 25 years unsuccessfully against the company tax lobby, which has been a complete swindle, but I've decided that I can't fight it any longer. So we might as well tidy it up and say that companies shan't pay a lot of tax. But let's simplify it; let's have a dividend tax, and a payroll tax and get rid of all these silly calculations. In 1948, I think, I was the first advocate - I published a paper in 1948 when Beveridge was plain 'Bill' (not Sir William or Lord) - on negative income tax, which was the ideal. But there were obvious difficulties, so I've come down to something much simpler. I have suggested that companies should pay the whole of what is called National Insurance as a payroll tax, but simply having it based upon the whole payroll - not knocked off at a certain level.

You think companies should pay? You are excluding partnerships and non-incorporated businesses?

No, I'm saying it should be taxed on companies, and it should be an allowable expense for anybody else. Going back to the 1950s, Beveridge was a friend of mine. The only company that he ever joined was my [British] Gas Light Company. I don't know whether you know this part of the story?

I'd like to know.

I was in on the birth of PAYE. There were two systems. I was on the British Employers Confederation's Tax Committee.

As from what dates?

This is going back to 1943, when PAYE was born. There was a completely new class of income tax payer during the war - the weekly wage earner, who had never paid tax before. Paul Chambers, a very bright Secretary to the Inland Revenue, suddenly found himself with a £100 million pounds of [tax] arrears that he could not claim. So he got this PAYE system. Whether he invented it or not, I don't know - whether he did it personally, or whether somebody did it for him.

He has been credited with it, certainly.

He sold it very brilliantly to the TUC, and of course gave away all the concessions that have been so difficult - automatic refunds during absence, and so on, whether it was to do with strikes, or sickness, or unemployment. Now, having sold a pup, he said to the TUC: 'Look, boys, let's make life simple for your boys in future; I'll cancel these arrears', not telling the Board [of Inland Revenue] or the TUC that he had not a cat in hell's chance of collecting them anyway. Anyway, having sold them a pup, he then came to the British Employer's Confederation and wasn't prepared to budge an inch. And a couple of very brilliant actuaries, Curtin and Haines, put up an alternative scheme which was much simpler for the employers to operate, and tore that [other scheme] to pieces.

I was then representing the building trade and the public works contractors, and we were not organised as at present; we couldn't get annual [running] totals every week from our employees. We wanted something simpler. So I put forward what was a modified scheme. We did it on a weekly basis, and every three or four weeks you did an accumulation. I deliberately made sure that when you did your accumulation you had a little bit of tax to pay back [to the employee], because you couldn't go back and collect any more. Therefore Paul Chambers, and Willis [of the TUC], who became very friendly with both of us - they tore my pants off on the basis that it was a scheme of consistent over-production. And I went home that night very angry. You know, when you've been put through the mangle by experts, you feel a bit ragged. So I went back to my office; I collected all the documents including the debates in the House [of Commons] and the White Paper, and I took them home. And I told my wife: 'make me a flask of coffee, and go to bed. I'm not coming to bed'.

And I started browsing, and suddenly I found myself asking, as I looked at the White Paper and its illustration: 'Why the hell does he always pay on Monday and Tuesday? I've not known that in industry!' And suddenly the penny dropped. If he paid on the normal Thursday or Friday, he came up against a horrid 53rd week and so on. I had found his Achilles'

Heel. So I sat down and composed a letter to *The Financial News*, as it was, which was supporting my scheme. It later became amalgamated with *The Financial Times*. Having written the letter, I then sat back - it was now about 5 o'clock in the morning. I then sat back and said: 'Well, it won't do any good to get this letter published, but let's play some mental chess.' What happens if, first thing in the morning, I ring up the chairman of the British Employers Federation and say: 'Sir, as a matter out of courtesy, I will redo this letter before I take it round. I think, you see, you can't do this thing without me talking to Chambers'. So I did this, and he agreed, and so I said: 'Very well, so I'll bring the letter to your office'.

So he rang up Chambers, and Chambers hesitated a few minutes and said: 'Well, let's have another meeting', and he agreed my scheme - not on its merits (although it had merits): he did not want the other scheme. And in fact the other bit of luck I had was that, using his own illustrations, my scheme, as he said, was consistently nearer the actual Act of Parliament than his scheme was. And so it was agreed; and I carried it on. Actually, I invented a tax slide which produced, within a matter of seconds, what took several minutes by hand.

I can see why, clearly, from the point of view of the building employees there were special problems, and they needed advice on that. Your career was within that industry? How had you originally qualified?

Oh, I qualified and I took an industrial job immediately.

So you qualified with whom?

A little firm called Alfred Nixon, Son & Turner. Then I took a commercial job which I didn't like very much, and I decided to go back into the profession, into the big league. I went into [Thomson] McLintock and became chief clerk in Manchester. And then I took a step out at a much higher level. I became chief accountant to John Mowlem, the builders in London, and that is where I was when PAYE started.

And then when the incompetent sons of directors were being put over my head onto the Board, I decided I'd keep my powder dry. I'd made a national reputation with my PAYE, you see. I think I was getting on fairly well in the profession, and what I wanted to do was to get on the board of a public company. The offer came from Rediffusion, and I took it on.

So, to get the perspective right, you went to Thomson McLintock in what - about the mid 1930s?

I qualified in 1928. Either 1929 or 1930 - I think it would be 1929; and I was with him for about 9 years. I finished up as chief clerk in Manchester, with a sort of Field Marshall's baton in my nap-sack. Well, it is very interesting. When I was chief clerk in Manchester, Bill Slimmings [later President of the Scottish Institute] was chief clerk in London.

Oh, was he?

And we met together on floating Lancashire Steel Company. I knew I could get the partnership there, but this offer came out of the blue. I had done the job before. I had done a very good job, and the bloke did a good job in inviting me to London to become chief accountant of Mowlem's.

Well, 1938 was a pretty difficult time?

1937.

1937 was a pretty difficult time to go down to London, just on the eve of war, wasn't it, with the building industry facing complete disruption to their pattern of working.

Oh, you were responsible for the maintenance of the sewers, the docks and one or two other things.

You mentioned the sewers; it must have been an incredibly difficult job with bombs falling.

Oh yes, we built a shelter, you know, quite a good shelter. Had a bomb hit it, I suppose it wouldn't have done any good, but we spent a little time in there. We spent one night there, fire watching. One incredible thing during the war is with what little sleep you could manage. I only had four nights in bed a week. I had one night fire watching at the office, one night in the Home Guard, and one night fire watching. And I didn't leave my office before midnight. I was involved in the organisation up to the fall of France, and then I was involved in the great operation digging the defence lines.

Yes. Somebody else in the same industry at that time was Harry Norris; did you know Harry Norris?

Harry? Oh, yes; he is an old friend of mine.

I think I ought to have a word with him at some stage; he did some interesting stuff on inflation accounting.

Well, there was a bunch of us who formed this Luncheon Club.

Now, that is one of the things I very much wanted to ask you about. The Luncheon Club is a fairly famous institution, and I'd like to find

out a little bit more about the Luncheon Club. And there was also The 1949 Group; were you involved in that?

The 1949 Group? I think it is the same: it was the same mob wasn't it?

Well, they met in the evenings, The 1949 Group, whereas the Luncheon Club was clearly a matter of lunching. You formed this Luncheon Club with Harry Norris?

Well, the three moving spirits - I think the three moving spirits, were Ian Davison, Joe Latham and myself.

Ian Davidson - he must have been very young at that time.

No, not that one - Eric Davidson. We fought the Institute; we fought the Council for membership and fellowship in the late 1940s and early 1950s. And the final decision was five [members] - and five only. They accepted me because they thought I was safer in than out!

Yes. On the formation of this Luncheon Club, this would have been about this time - 1943 or thereabouts?

Oh, no; it was later than 1943 - it was the late 40s. When was Gilbert Shepherd the President [of the ICAEW]? I think the revision of the charter was agreed by Shepherd; he was 1947/8. I believe it was agreed to by Shepherd, and that was about the time of the formation of the Luncheon Club and the 1949 Club?

It was a very stimulating and informative time; it was a most exciting time from my point of view as a historian. There were so many ideas in flux between 1940 - well, in fact the whole of the war time period.

Well, it really went back to a famous general meeting during the war. It finished with a scrum on the stairs, and it had to be adjourned to Grosvenor House. There was great dissatisfaction with the training provided for the students, and it led finally to the formation of the Taxation & Research Committee; that is where it all started from.

Well, that was 1942 - the formation of the T&FR [Taxation and Financial Relations Committee].

Now then; I'm trying to think - yes, I think Palmour was President when we had the famous adjourned meeting. There was a scrum on the stairs, and I was pulled half way up the stairs. There was an adjourned meeting, and there was the formation of the Taxation and Research Committee. The leading figure really was old de Paula, Frederick de Paula. And, unhappily, he was drummed off the Council a few years later, by reason of the Carr-Saunders Report on Education. He was a great educationalist, apart from being a great accountant.

He held the part-time chair at LSE, didn't he, by that stage?

Yes. Well, he was a great educationalist in his own right, and he was put on the Carr-Saunders Committee, which was a great committee on education. About 1944, I think. No, it was after the war - 1945 or 1946. Anyway, he was put on it in his own right, just before he was put on the Council; and he was put on the Council, again on his own merits, before we got this general acknowledgement for non-practising accountants. Unfortunately, one of his greatest virtues wasn't always tact; he was deputy chairman of this Committee and he did two rather stupid things - one in particular. When the 'Big-wigs' from the Institute went to give evidence, Carr-Saunders was not available, and de Paula took the chair and he put them through their paces.

And the other thing he did that was a bit tactless was that he signed the report, which was very critical of the Institute's so called educational and training, without any discussion at all with the President. Now, I'm very mindfully aware of this. There was a vicious - I think the report was round about 1950 - there was an infamous pamphlet, written by Wilkinson [Secretary of the ICAEW], really hounding de Paula for his part in this, as a result of which he was rubbed off the Council. Now, the reason why I'm so familiar with this is that the committee was resurrected ten years later as the McMeeking Committee, and I was the one who was put on [to represent the ICAEW].

There was a very bright boy at the Ministry [of Education] who went right to the top, you know; he wasn't in the higher ranks of the Ministry then, but he became 'Sir Anthony' Park, with all the 'gongs' that go with it. He became number one of the industry; he was bright, but then he was just 'Anthony Park, OBE', I think. He was obviously very bright. He rang up the Secretary and said: 'Look, I'd like a member of your Council - somebody fairly valuable', or something like that. And the next thing I knew, I was on this committee. So I rang up the Secretary [of the ICAEW] and said: 'Hey, I know how you got rid of de Paula: is this my exit?' He said: 'Oh, I suggested you because you're the best tight rope walker on the Council'.

We had just set up the Parker Committee to look into educational matters [at the ICAEW], and so at the first meeting [of the McMeeking Committee] I argued like hell to exclude ourselves, and so as not to be too obvious, by reason of parity I got the Law Society excluded too because of their use of the pupillage method. And then I could say what the hell I wanted - as a result of which, of course, I talked myself onto the drafting committee. And then when we got the outline of the draft report, prepared by the Ministry of Education boys, I was so appalled at their form of reporting that I said to the chairman: 'Look, old boy - give me a week and I'll re-write this bloody thing'. So I wrote the whole summary of conclusions and recommendations. McMeeking was a very good chairman, and he said very little at the meetings except, after an hour and 25 minutes, he would look at his watch and say: 'Look gentlemen, it is time we settled a time and place for the next meeting'. So he was a very good chairman. And also he sold his quality as chairman; he altered half of one sentence [in the report] to make sure it was a committee thing and not just a one-man thing.

The amusing thing is that I've just had, as a result of this, a hell of a battle with the local authority over the education of my granddaughter who lives with us. She spent most of the time at the French Lycee, and then when they came to A-levels she wanted to become a vet. She and I decided the Lycee wasn't too good on the science side, but there is a very good science college just within a mile and a half of our house - but it happens to be just on the wrong side of the Surrey border. Surrey is fighting all the London Boroughs because, under pressure from the Ministry of Education to cut down their spending, instead of sacking their surplus teachers they thought it would be a good idea to refuse to pay for their pupils who are coming to London colleges. Instead of twisting the minister's arm under the Education Act to make them toe the line, they [the London Borough of Sutton Education Authority] said: 'Oh, well - boo to you: we won't pay for people going to your colleges', despite the fact there isn't a college in Sutton with a science course that my granddaughter wanted. I had a hell of a fight, and I quoted the fact that I'd written the blasted report which said 'this is the way that mutual co-operation was the basis of existence for further education'.

I had to pay over £1,000 a year to get my granddaughter to the nearest state college, but I got most of it back. Actually, I shamed Surrey themselves into repaying it because I suddenly discovered that if she were normally resident in Omsk, or Timbuctoo, or New York she would come in on a 10% rate [laugh]. So when I found that out, Surrey hadn't much hope.

Yes; where is this college that she is staying?

Ewell - the North East College of Technology; it is only a mile and a half from my house. Sutton would have paid any London Borough, but they wouldn't pay Surrey. Actually I got 7/8ths of my money back, but I'm carrying on the fight on principle, and I've got an invitation to go and meet the head of the Surrey Education Department. And my own local MP, who I involved in the battle, is now a Minister of State of the Department of Education - so life is funny; life is full of fun.

Now what is the form of the book you're writing?

Well, there has been no history written from this period from 1935 up to 1950 in terms of an analysis of where ideas came from - how they came to develop, and the various influences such as the effect of inflation and the effects of the government's development role particularly in the war time period, and the leading figures, the personalities involved, the formative ideas and so on.

Well, you realise inflation has been a one-man fight against 67, don't you? I wrote something for the *Financial Times* which they rejected; indeed, I thought I'd take advantage of your facilities to get a copy of that [indicating a draft letter] off to *The Accountant*.

Yes; you are welcome to do that. It is interesting that there has been so little written.

Well, I've written a hell of a lot. When I go travelling, I travel light you see. I usually bring my latest [National Expenditure] 'Blue Book'; my national income and expenditure accounts, my latest copy of *Economic Trends* and my latest copy of the Budget.

Now, let's go back a bit. You were involved with the British Employers' Confederation. When Stafford Cripps was Chancellor of the Exchequer in 1947 and 1948, he spoke in his budget speeches of the need for British industry to re-equip, and said that there had been representations to him by the FBI. And he tried to get parallel working parties set up by the FBI and the TUC, but I never saw anything come out of that.

No. Anderson did something; Anderson was the first man to do something.

What is his initial - which Anderson?

He was the Chancellor - he became Lord Anderson. Anderson, when he was in Churchill's war-time government, he introduced something just towards the end of the war, in 1944 I think. He introduced some special capital allowance - that was the first of it. And then in 1951, they had one of these professors go through the accounts of a group of companies between 1938 and 1948, and it was very interesting. It was a summary of their assets, and his conclusion was their profits hadn't been excessive - and there was no reference to profits at all in the study. He said it was clear that prices and profits were not excessive, and I had a bash at it in my 1952 paper entitled 'Are the figures any use?'

Right. This was in *The Accountant?*

In, *The Accountant* in 1952.

Yes. 1952 was a very extraordinary year. There were so many things. The Cost & Works published a book on replacement cost accounting.

The Association of Certified & Corporate Accountants published a very important book.

The reason for it was that we rushed out the famous *Recommendation N15* because of the international conference [the 1952 International Congress of Accountants, in London] where it was tabled.

Right - the conference.

Now there was a great American accountant - an English/American accountant - who developed the concept … now what was his beautiful concept? I met him in London shortly beforehand. He had a lovely concept to justify it.

Not George May?

George May: that is right. I'd argued it out with him. I met him on the stairs and I said: 'Sir, are you going to speak on this?'. He said: 'Young man, I shall deal with your silly argument!'. The 'Postulate of Permanence', that was it. George May's Postulate of Permanence. Have you got the 1952 conference - the Sixth International Conference?

No, I don't have the proceedings. I use the library copy.

Well, if you look at the library copy, you'll see how I tore his pants off, because I dealt with the postulate of permanence - the life of man is sufficiently impermanent. And then I quoted our mortality statistics compared with the mortality statistics of companies, which were lying. Poor old George May; when he got onto the platform, he put his notes in his pocket and said: 'After this conference, I'll be able to deal with some of these specious arguments'. [Laughter] And one of my expressions went down with a bang. I said: 'This replacement cost accounting just amounts to fig leaves with which to cover up something', and it went down with a bang, actually. You see, I'd been deeply involved in this because in 1948/49 I was chairman of the Taxation & Research Committee: that is when we fought it all out.

I see. Well, that is interesting.

And from that moment I had attacked the new accounting, not in essence but as a tax fiddle.

I see, yes.

Now, we killed it in 1952. Now at the next conference, four years later, I attacked Parker. He was a Council member and a future president.

W. E. - Bill - Parker?

Yes, W.E. Parker. I attacked him because, instead of defending *Recommendation 15*, he went and criticised it at the next conference, so I attacked him. And the amusing thing was that in 1957, the great Henry Benson was brought onto the Council and he was made chairman of the committee - chairman of the Joint Representatives - to squash me, because they were going to produce something on replacement cost accounting. And I killed it stone dead with one letter: I quote that letter in my 1971 paper called 'Inflation and Accounts', in which really I libelled every member of the Council. I challenged them - oh yes, this is where your professor came in [Edward Stamp]. He said some very rude words in Saxon about me in *Accountancy Age*, and I wrote a reply in *The Accountant* addressing thirteen questions and challenging him to answer them. It has got to the point that no member of Council, nobody will take me up on them because I used to finish with my pants on. Your worthy professor didn't answer any of my thirteen questions.

You ought to write him a letter, putting it in black and white in a letter to him and saying 'please can I have a reply?' - because that undoubtedly would be what he would do if he sent a letter and didn't get a reply.

No: I published it, and I was content that he didn't reply. And no member of Council did either. Well, it was defamatory. I said they'd betrayed the Institute.

Yes, I remember this.

But I do it on the basis that they don't want to sue me. [Laughter] They don't want me in the witness box.

Yes [laugh]. Your opposition to current value accounting is primarily from the point of view of tax?

That it is a tax fiddle. As soon as I saw Sandilands, I said this is fine.

You like Sandilands?

Oh, yes. In fact - who was it? - Peter Shore in presenting it to parliament said that you get a better view of the economic performance of companies. Well, going back 25 years, when I was comptroller of Rediffusion, I always used to prepare my budgets in two columns: current prices and historical prices. That is going back a quarter of a century ago.

Did you? Well, that is not the impression that I got from one or two things I've seen of yours. Your reference to 'funny money', for example, suggests that you were concerned for a current purchasing power adjustment - an ED8 type of adjustment.

No. Current cost accounting is right.

Yes, you used a currency unit without re-stating it in terms of units constant purchasing power and whatever.

No. What I've said is that you can do both. I've written: 'If any board wishes to express results in terms of money in real terms, I see no reason why on earth they should not do so'. The best solution is possibly a combination of Sandilands for the accounts and further adjustments.

I merely attack this as part of the company tax lobby. I've always said Sandilands is right. I took an awful lot of trouble. I stuck my neck out in my 'Eureka' paper by taking the VAT accounts and 'doing a Sandilands' on it, you see, and that is the right answer, without any inside know-how. Before I published it, one of my friends, one of the finance directors, invited me to lunch with two finance directors, their chief accountant and their professional auditor, and just put me through the mill. And they couldn't find anything much wrong with it. If anything stinks you just tell me. I've stuck my neck out in order to defend Sandilands. That was the first defence, and in the 'Eureka' one, I said: 'Look, this is how you can combine the two'. I've written so many of the damned things. I've written masses. In fact, a friend of mine who knew somebody from one of the Ministries who deals with this said to him: 'You know Jack Clayton?' he replied: 'Oh my God I've got a file that big - and half of it is on Jack Clayton'.

Did you get involved at all with the Accounting Research Association when that was set up in the war?

No.

Where did this [1949] lunch club come from, then? Was this because you were working in those days with Eric [Hay] Davidson?

This arose from the pressure to get recognition for the industrial accountant, both recognition as Council members and recognition as Fellows [rather than merely Associates]; that is how it really arose. I mean, those of us who were involved just popped around and found some of the leading industrial accountants in London. Harry Norris was one; Basil Smallpeice was one - although he was opposed to us at the beginning. He came round at the finish.

Were you in touch at all with the academic people? With de Paula and Baxter? Baxter was a member of the Scottish Institute of course.

No. I don't think de Paula was a member.

Was Lawrence Robson involved?

No, it was industrial accountants only. Robson was in practice.

He was in practice, but I was wondering whether his consulting side - whether he was involved because of his interest in standard costing and these things. He would have been a fairly natural ally, I would have thought, to have pushed the practising rights.

There was a rather interesting book on standard costing produced by the T&FR Committee. Have you see that?

Yes, I have. A very interesting book.

I was involved in that.

Very interesting. That came out about 1949 or 1950.

And, of course, the refresher courses inspired by de Paula were a very important step. Just after the war.

These were the Oxford ones?

No, I think the refresher course was a booklet, but the lectures were given at Cambridge. I gave two of them. I gave one on mechanised accounting. That is worth looking at. In 1948. It was very interesting. I put at the head of my paper, when I first looked at it, 'The Philosophy of Mechanisation' - and I hadn't the courage, so when I finally did it I called it 'Principles of Mechanisation'. *The Accountant* took it as the bases of their leading article with the title 'The Philosophy of Mechanisation'.

What an extraordinary thing.

Yes, I was groping for [the idea of] a computer, in 1948 I think it would have been.

Good heavens. Going back to your career, you spent some years with Mowlem's.

Nine years, and then I went to Rediffusion. I think it was about 1946.

That must have been quite a small company in those days.

Yes. I helped to build it up. In fact, commercial television was floated on my desk - as to what it would do.

And are you pleased to see the second [TV] channel?

I'm pleased. I'm pleased it is not going to the BBC, for the reason of public expenditure as much as anything else.

That [working in Rediffusion] would have presented quite different sorts of accounting problems, wouldn't it, as opposed to Mowlem's, where you were concerned for a lot of contract accounting. You were there over the war time period - you were scarcely with Mowlem's outside the war period.

Yes. I was there from just when the war was starting - you know, when the build up was starting to the war until just after the end of the war.

Yes. So at that stage you would have been heavily involved with government contracting and negotiating and this sort of thing?

Yes, very much so.

Did this have a significant effect on accounting ideas and thinking? The impact of negotiation with government?

OK, it is a great shame that integration [of the professional accountancy bodies] was sabotaged because if you had one solitary profession you could blackball employers and trade unions too. And until you get to that position I don't think you can possibly exert discipline.

Now, talking about sabotaging integration, what did go wrong with integration? How was it stopped? The integration of the Society [of Incorporated Accountants and Auditors with the ICAEW] had gone through as a result of some hard bargaining. What was your view at that stage in 1957?

Well, wait a minute. The Integration Committee [for the integration of the SIAA and the ICAEW] comprised about a dozen practising members and one non-practising member.

With the Society?

Yes, yes. One non-practising member - me. My original reaction was 'anti': why the hell should we give it away? But we had a very fine chairman in Bill Lawson, who knew me very well. He didn't seek to argue with my views. I wrote him a letter saying: 'Look, Bill, why the hell should we give all this away?' And Bill just wrote me a very nice letter saying 'well, have you thought of this? Have you thought of that? Have you thought of that?' He was very tactful and a very fine accountant, was Bill. And I reflected, and I came to this conclusion. I was rather proud of the fact we had no barriers of sex, race, colour or creed - but we had a cash barrier, and this would destroy the cash barrier. So I finally came round to the idea that it was the right thing to do. But the interesting thing was when we presented it to the Council. I said to the Council: 'Look, gentlemen, you do understand that eventually this means you'll have to pay a living wage to your articled clerks'. How I was right! They now get about two or three thousand a year.

Two is the minimum, yes. And the Society had some pretty strong people on their side at that time, didn't they?

Oh, there is no doubt about it. It was the right thing to do had we done the complete integration [of all six major bodies in the 1960s]. It was during Stanley Dixon's time [as President of the ICAEW], and two members sabotaged it. And one I've spoken to since said he was rather sorry on reflection that he had done so.

Really!

Yes, it was a great shame. It has now led to this, all these composite groups.

All busy working in different directions, yes.

Yes. The CCAB, and so on. In fact there is a letter of mine in *The Accountant* somewhere saying: 'We ought to take them by the scruff of their neck - we ought to form the Royal Institute of Chartered Accountants, and we ought to start it off and invite them [all] to join in'. I said this some years ago. I think it is a great shame.

The issues in the 1960s over the big integration were rather more difficult to resolve than with the Society.

No, there were no difficulties - it was just sheer sabotage. All the main bodies were agreed. It was simply sabotage by two of our members who got up a big propaganda campaign. It was a great shame yes. I'm trying to think - Hugh Nicholson and somebody else [in fact, Bruce Sutherland]. We let the whole profession down. Now we are suffering from it.

Yes, very much.

And they're fighting against hegemony.

Yes. Speaking for myself, I left school in 1957, and I'd had a look at chartered accountants' offices and decided I didn't like the auditing very much. So I went and trained with Dunlop's instead. So for that reason I qualified as a certified accountant, but for the life of me I don't see any justification in separate bodies - I really don't. I think there are one or two incidental advantages, but then there are a great deal more disadvantages. One advantage is, I think, that there is more

experimentation going on in training. I think that the Association's examination structure is probably somewhat better.

Yes, well I've always objected to this. I've quarrelled with many of my industrial friends. I'm very surprised that they are opposed to training in industry. I believe it is the job of any executive to train his successor. It is his first job, in my view, so he can be kicked upstairs. But so many people are so afraid of being kicked out. And I've always thought we should train chartered accountants both in industry and the profession - but they've got to spend some time in each.

Well, I found my training very good because it was clearly a different emphasis. I did not qualify as an auditor. I would not be an auditor. I would certainly have to do 30 months in an [auditing] office before I would feel that I could make a start with it. But it did mean to say that I got to know very well, after seven years or so, the workings of a major industrial group in Dunlop. And I'd met a lot of management and accounting problems - a lot of them management accounting problems and capital budgeting problems and so on.

The great advantage of a professional training is, I think, you'll see so many businesses, and I think you do - or should - get a facility of judgement on your own. Objectivity, really.

And it must have been this that was a major difficulty with integration wasn't it? Whether the training should have been within a practising office or not ….?

No, this was no problem I think. Ever since we had this the Parker Report, any idea of training in industrial offices has been turned down, but I was always in favour of it.

That is interesting. What about the idea of graduate entry to the profession?

Well, there has been a tremendous move towards it. I believe that most of the entrants now are graduates. A Council member was talking to my local group recently, and they are not too happy with the way things are going at the moment - particularly with the [high level of] failures in the final [examination]. I was disagreeing very violently with the views that they should have a period of work and then a separate period of study. I said they should organise things on a sandwich basis. I think you've got to have an integration of theory and practice all the time. The essence of education, I think, is bringing together theory and practice. To use de Paula's marvellous expression, 'education is rubbing brains together'.

He was an extraordinary mixture, de Paula, wasn't he because he was a good practitioner, he was a leading academic, and he was a very fine finance director of Dunlop's.

You have got his book haven't you?

We have it in the library, yes.

It is a very good book.

Yes. I want to go and see his son.

Yes. He was a great guy, was de Paula. My mentor.

Your mentor; how did that come about?

Well, we met on the T&FR Committee and I liked him immensely.

Yes - he was a vice chairman of the T&FR, wasn't he?

He was chairman at one time. He was the leading spirit behind me, really. It was lovely to hear the fighting between him and Rees.

P. M. Rees?

P. M. Rees - he was a great commercial accountant, at Unilever, in the early days. They were great days. P. M. Rees and - who was the chairman then?

They were fighting against each other? I would have thought ...

No, no - only 'rubbing brains'. Campbell was a very good member, too. He wrote a marvellous book on companies. Campbell was a very good member.

Do you know the name Lacey - K. Lacey?

Oh - it rings a bell, but I can't recall him. I think he has done a fair amount of writing.

He wrote some very important stuff in the 1940s, and then a book in 1952 published by Pitman's - *Accounting for Inflation*, or something of the sort.

There was a research bloke who did something on inflation, but they didn't like it because he was 'anti-current purchasing power' [laugh]. They quietly buried him. You know, the first thing that the Institute research boys did? I tore its pants off in *The Financial Times*. They portrayed a company whose cash assets exceeded its liabilities, and I just quoted from *The Annual Abstract of Statistics* - there 'ain't such a company!'.

Are you sympathetic with the idea of the monetary capital maintenance element in ED24? I've not read your letter in sufficient detail.

It is a fiddle.

I can see that from the banker's point of view. I just wondered whether you thought that there was some justification for a manufacturing concern?

No, none whatsoever. I mean this is why I say, look - Sandilands is very simple. Money is the unit of measurement, and assets and liabilities appear at a valuation - finish. It goes back to the *Spanish Prospecting Company* [law case]; you must remember the old conclusion - 'what is profit?' You take the assets at the beginning of a period, you take the assets at the end, you take the difference and you adjust it for capital put in or capital taken out - and that is profit. That is Sandilands - it is as simple as that. Monetary adjustment is a load of nonsense: it is a fiddle, and the big boys will always lead on the side of the big battalions.

It cost the insurance companies about one - I don't know whether it was 1, or 2 or 3 billion [pounds]. By the way, this old story of accountants going into industry to get a pension always amuses me. I've never taken a job with any pension rights. But I've never been in a job long without persuading the directors that they ought to have a pension scheme. My first one was a very primitive one with Mowlem's, which I hope they have improved since. It was insured with the Pru [Prudential Assurance], and when I left Mowlem's I had the right to take up a small policy, which I did.

That fell due in 1963, and I had a nice letter saying: 'Here is the amount of your policy, and here are the accumulated bonuses - and if you'll endorse your policy, we will send you a cheque'. So I sent a nice little letter back saying: 'Where is my share of capital profits?' And that brought on a lot of mail. After about a year's correspondence, they finally suggested I would like to meet one of their senior officials. It was my old friend Angus Murray, who was the investment manager with whom I'd done business. I said I'd be delighted to meet him, by which time they had changed their articles [Articles of Association]; they had started to distribute their capital profits for the first time. And by an accounting fiddle, the articles said that 95% at least of the profits must be distributed to the policy holders. And the way they'd covered that up was when they bought a share for a thousand pounds and sold it for two thousand and re-invested the two thousand, it was still recorded at the original cost of the original share. And I busted that. A few years ago, I was very amused to see the chairman of the Pru proudly saying that their terminal bonuses now were 75% of their annual bonuses - and I brought that in. I've had fun.

There is still, within insurance companies, an extraordinary problem in interpreting their accounts. It is quite impossible, it seems to me, to tell what profit is attributable to the shareholders, and what to the participating policy holders, and what part is being ploughed back for further growth or whatever - quite impossible to interpret insurance company accounts. We had an MA student here the year before last who wrote his dissertation, a short paper, on insurance company accounts, trying to compare the companies. They all use quite different bases. It is completely impossible to unravel what is happening to their proceeds, it seems to me.

Well, I am dragging them into the times [laugh]. I was told that if my stocking was long enough to go to the House of Lords [i.e. if he could fund the action], I could soon beat them.

Good gracious. That must have been very tempting, but it would have been a very, very expensive business - impossibly so.

Obviously. Well, I won the battle, very much like the one I am having with the education boys. I have got seven eighths of my money back and I'm just pursuing the principle that they should allow free exchange of students. I shall win that eventually.

In your view of company accounts, who do you think are the prime users? Who do you think company accounts should be designed for?

The shareholders.

Yes; you're not keen on the idea of them being designed for employees and all these other groups of people?

You said 'primarily'.

I did indeed - deliberately so.

Certainly. I think they've got horribly complicated over the years. There was a very fine symposium done - when were group accounts brought in?

By Dunlop's, in 1931 for the first time.

No - the Act: when did the Companies Act require them?

Well, there was provision in the 1929 Act, but it was not operable until the 1948 Act.

Round about 1950, after the consolidated accounts had been put into the Act, the London District Society had three of its members along to make presentations. Percy Rees was one, and they had an excellent discussion.

What is an anathema to me is standard costing, as you call it now. It makes life much too complicated.

I did a very big paper on the future of the Institute. This was in the days you see, going back many years now, when the post-war Labour Government was handing out money lavishly for education. I said: 'We ought to build up our own university of accounting with houses in all the main areas of population, and the whole question of accounting recommendation should be de-centralised to the local society, to work in association with the universities'.

Good gracious, I never knew that. I didn't associate that with you. I've heard that people like Bertram Nelson were very interested indeed to build up working relationship with the universities.

It was a huge document. I was convalescing, and I called it 'The Idle Thoughts of an Idle Fellow' [laugh]. I went into great detail as to the future of the profession. I wrote about 18 pages. I started up in Westmoreland, I called in Manchester, and I finished it at the Institute. And then I summarised it.

This idea of standardisation is bloody nonsense in my view. You see, Hegel said it all. You cannot standardise accounting. A few weeks ago, there was a man quoting from fifty years' experience as a chartered accountant, and he said that everything is changing. The idea of *Recommendations* is fine - you can look at the recommendation and take account of what has happened since. And anyway you want multiple recommendations. But the idea of standards, to try and put accounting into a straight jacket, is nonsense because conditions differ from company to company.

Certainly what one needs, surely, is not so much a prescriptive formula - 'this is what you will do' - but some statement of the reasoning; just what are our priorities, and what is it that we are seeking to show?

Well, this is what we used to do with our accounting *recommendations*. I think the Taxation & Research Committee did a marvellous job. But the reason - I've said all this in print - the reason for the standards largely is the elephantine development of the bigger firms, side by side with the tremendous concentration of industry. They have become too big, really. And it is the way of the pardoners, do you see; before they can sign on the dotted line, they want to know that every 't' has been crossed and every 'i' dotted. It destroys initiative, you see. It must lower the competence and the whole tone of the profession.

Well, there is no doubt that the profession these days uses audit manuals in such detail - everything is pre-planned before anyone leaves the office. There is certainly no discretion left, I'd have thought, for integration [of the profession].

Well, let me give you an example of the sort of thing that happened in my youth that would be impossible today. One of the greatest accountants of his day was of course Sir William McLintock, when I was chief clerk in 1930. These are the days before the merchant banker became supreme. The top accountant was supreme, and he used his friendly relations with the chairman of ICI, I think it was McGowan. And he rang me one day from London; it was late one Friday afternoon, and he said: 'By the way, McGowan's just been on the phone to me'. I think it was McGowan. 'There is a rumour on the news networks today that ICI are going to buy the Salt Union' - the people who dig most of the salt, out Northwich way. He said: 'Now, he wants it settled within a week so I want you to go on Monday morning, to Northwich, and I want you here next Thursday morning with the report and evaluation. And you haven't enough staff in Manchester. You just ring me back within half an hour to tell me how many staff you want sent up to the Midland Hotel from London. And I want that report'.

Those were my instructions. And I rang him back ten minutes later and said: 'Sir William, I don't want any staff'. He said: 'don't be silly - you haven't enough staff'. I said: 'it is impossible - we cannot do it with any staff. We cannot go into an organisation 100 years old, you tell me, and after several re-organisations and amalgamations. It is impossible: we can't find our way around. You've told me the name of the secretary. If he is a straight shooter, I will use his staff. If he pulls my leg once, I'll walk out; if he plays the game, you'll have your report'. That is precisely what I did. Now can you imagine that in a book on the standard technique?

No, it simply couldn't be done.

That was the good old days. That is when accounting was accounting. And I was there with my evaluation, and that was the basis on which the deal was done.

Yes. It couldn't be done now, very largely because of the threat of law suits.

No. I'll tell you another incident, which sent them round the bend. I'd spoken to Joe Latham and Bill.....

Latham, of AEI?

Yes. Now Sir Joseph Latham - who worked side by side with me in Manchester for many years. The reason I know he is such a good accountant is that I took over his job when he left.

Was he with Thomson McLintock?

Yes. And Bill Slimmings. He was doing the London end, I was doing the steel end, and Latham was doing the coal end of a big amalgamation. For half a million pounds, the Bank of England got control of Lancashire Steel and Wigan Coal, in the dismal 1930s. And just as it was going through, Bill Slimmings got on the phone to me and said: 'Look, this can't go through for three months, and we have got to have a budget to say the company can stay solvent for three months - and you'd better get them cracking on it'. So I went to see Andrew White, who was a chartered accountant and the managing director, and I said: 'This is what they want - you'd better get cracking quick'. So a few days later, he presented me with a budget showing a few pounds left in the kitty, and I had a good look at it. I said: 'Plus or minus a quarter of a million [pounds]', and he said, 'I agree'. He said: 'But I'll be here, I promise you'. On that promise I signed up.

And then the next thing that happened was that we suddenly found that one of the companies had had an old fashioned form of engagement document which they'd signed, promising their staff a ten bob a week pension after so many years. And I got that valued - that was at least half a million. I then had another session with Andrew White; we sacked the bloody lot and re-engaged them the next day. He and I decided it; we didn't refer it to London - we just decided it was the only way. Those were the days!

There is a big row, of course, now on the question of accounting for pension costs. There is a very interesting development that is taking place just at the moment, on how to account for the pensions costs in the published accounts. The way in which it is going at the moment is that it is going to rely entirely on actuarial valuations. This is one of the very few areas in accounting where the standard - which is at the exposure draft stage at the moment - is asking for forecasts about the future very explicitly. Since accounts have always been very much on the basis of history of the past and never predictions of the future, this is going to open a flood gate.

After I had retired, I was invited by the Plessey boys to go and do a management audit for them, which was great fun. And one of the problems we had - I had a hell of a fight with their company secretary, Haydn Guest, on pensions. We disagreed violently, but he was on the committee of the National Pensions Association, and suddenly he came to me one day and he said: 'Look, we have just been let down for our annual meeting. Harold Wincott should have given us a paper, but he has found he is double-dated. He has got a date in America, and he prefers that one - he gets better expenses'. He said: 'look, I don't agree with your views on pensions, but they are quite interesting; would you come and give us a paper?' Well, I'm not an expert on pensions, but you know I can't resist a challenge like that. So I got up in front of all these members, about a thousand experts. They are all the leading insurance people, all the actuaries - the lot. And I stuck my neck out. And one of the strongest views I expressed is that I'm root and branch opposed to terminal salary pensions, on the grounds that no director of a company has the right to issue post-dated cheques of an unknown amount - least of all a government minister. And how right I was!

Obviously, the thing to do is to insure it.

You can't insure it.

Insurance policies. Assurance policies.

You can't insure a terminal salary pension.

Not a terminal salary. I'm saying that the answer is to take out policies.

The solution, which I tried at our television company, was a money purchase scheme. You insure the amount payable on death; you invest the remainder. But what you do is you have elected trustees from the staff on a 50/50 basis, and you promise them that any surplus will be used to augment the pensions. And when you've got a surplus, then you declare a dividend - you say pensions go up 20, 30, 40, 50%. This is the way to do it. This is what I said at the time. And this is, oh, 10 or 15 years ago. Now Barclays Bank put in 45% or something [to their final salary pensions scheme], and it still isn't enough. And this bloody fool Barbara Castle has put a millstone round the government's neck. I'm hoping this government will change that [Pensions] Act.

They are not going to be able to do it retrospectively.

Oh no, I agree. But the only way to deal with state pensions, in my view, is to have them at fixed amounts. I don't think they should commit themselves to ordinary state pensions rising at a fixed percentage. I think each year they should look at the economy and say: 'Right, pensions all round can go up by X%'.

Yes. It would be very nice to index link it with a general price level.

Well, that is what is causing inflation.

Quite so, yes. All you get then is a time lagged effect where last period's inflation goes through into this period's crisis.

Well, where is the professor [Eddie Stamp] - is he in today?

No, he is not. He is in London today, unfortunately. I'll probably see him later on today.

I'm sorry I missed him.

Well, he tends to plan a long way ahead, necessarily. I haven't seen him in fact for a couple of days.

How big is your unit here?

Well, we have a staff of about 15 within the Department. And then the International Centre for Research & Accounting has got a variable number of people who are mostly working on a part-time basis. At the moment, I think, the full-time staff here is only two, but there are quite a number of people who are visiting scholars in one capacity or another.

Yes. And how are you financed?

Well, the great majority of us who are in the Department, of course, are financed by the UGC through the university. The Research Centre itself has raised its own finances. It was set up originally by the Rank Foundation, which set up its initial endowment, and then it has augmented by private donations, endowments from outside. So the Research Centre itself doesn't come out of the university funds at all, whereas the Department, of course, the rest of us, we have got a teaching load. Our bread and butter is primarily earned by teaching students - very, very large numbers of students.

Teaching them what?

Degrees in accounting and finance, mainly. First and foremost, a three year undergraduate degree, and a very intensive 12 month MA.

What are they - BA or BSc?

It is a BA, generally.

BA Com - is it BA Com?

No, it is just a Bachelor of Arts degree in accounting and finance. And then there is a combined degree in economics with accountancy. 'Economics and Financial Control', it is called, but it is a title we are about to drop. And then they can do a certain amount of other subjects in different degree combinations. They can do some marketing, or some operational research or some work in industrial relations.

Yes, who was head of Ranks - who is it that is retired there? An old associate of mine. You mean Ranks the picture people, not Ranks the mill owners.

The Rank Organisation - that is right, yes. Sir John Davis.

John Davis. Was it John Davis who did it?

As far as I'm aware - I think it was, yes.

Did he get an honorary degree for it?

He doesn't hold an honorary degree from this university. Sir Ronald Leach does.

What has he done to deserve that?

I know that he was obviously heavily involved with the process of the Accounting Standards Committee …

… which was a tragedy…

… and some time after that the Research Centre was set up, and he was helpful in that process too. There is quite a lot of ……

What was he? Doctor of Law or something?

Yes. There is quite a distinguished list of Trustees in the Research Centre.

They're the ones who give out the honorary degrees, are they?

No. That has to come through the university - it is the university's decision, a decision of the Senate. As a department we are suffering very much from the fact that the department was set up in 1968, it really grew fast as from about 1972.

Switch this off. [Tape recorder off for several minutes]

But I've done my own private studies, you see, and I've written a lot of papers, mostly in *The Accountant*. I've made them set up this new series. I've now got an argument - I've got a very interesting argument with the national income accounts. You can try your logical mind on this. Are you familiar with the national income accounts?

I have a nodding acquaintance with them - I don't know them in detail.

Well, I'll show you something very interesting. Are you familiar with the concept of GDP and GNP at factor cost?

Yes.

Right; you know how they get their expenditure total and then they deduct a factor cost adjustment - they deduct taxation, rent subsidies and so on.

Right - transfer payments.

Yes. They have a little table in which they analyse these; they get the total tax less subsidies and they analyse this against consumer spending, government direct spending, gross capital formation and exports. OK?

Yes.

Now then, I've been arguing, and I'm just going back to re-argue, with Jack Hibbert who is the chief statistical officer on national accounts, that that figure which is now about £1½ billions a year - that it should be added, they should not deduct it from the GNP; it is a government export of services. We have been paid that from abroad, and I think the GNP is under-stated, to a tidy and logical mind.

I know somebody who would be interested in that argument and that is Basil Yamey, at the London School of Economics.

Well, I'll write it up in *The Accountant*.

He is very, very interested in national income accounting. He thinks that there is a tremendous amount of improvement that is needed.

[J.R.] Hicks, and [J.R.N.] Stone and Sewell Bray did some useful
pioneering work in the 1940s...

Yes, I remember Sewell Bray.

Do you?

Yes; he took the job I turned down. I was invited to go and clean up
the British interests in Egypt after the Suez War.

Good gracious!

I sat down and wrote a thesis on the Middle East for the Foreign Office.
I said it was quite hopeless for an Englishman to go and settle by way of
a bond in an Egyptian village the English claims in that village. I would
very happily agree for an Egyptian to meet me anywhere but in Egypt.
I'd be very happy to do this on a global basis, and everybody could send
in claims - they could settle it, agree the claims and marry them up with
a global settlement. He was very interested, the top Foreign Office man I
saw. I said, I wouldn't take it on the basis they wanted, but I would take
it on this basis, and he said the only settlements that had been made at
all had been on a global basis. But what they wanted, in my view, was
a cat's paw. They wanted to say: 'Well, we sent out this distinguished
accountant' - that sort of thing. And I wasn't playing that game. But
it was very amusing.

When was this? 1957/58?

Oh no, it was after I retired. It was in the early 1960s. And I said it was
the focal point of one the world's greatest conflicts. I've still got it [the
thesis] at home. The night after the interview, I sat down and wrote a
thesis on the conflict of politics in the Middle East. It was a nice job.

I could have it on my own terms, take my wife, paid, set my own pace, everything I wanted. I was sorry to turn it down.

And Sewell Bray went?

I think Sewell Bray took it. I'm almost sure it was Sewell Bray.

What did you feel about the Stamp Martin Chair after the Institute and the Society had merged? Because the journal *Accounting Research* **ceased publication at that stage, and I understand Stamp Martin Chair was suspended wasn't it?**

Well, I'm sorry - I don't remember it …… it doesn't ring much of a bell.

There was a professorship which Sewell Bray held at the Society's Hall.

That is right.

…and that terminated in 1957. Nothing ever happened to it after that. I think clearly the funds just stopped and that was the end of it He presumably just went back to Tansley Witt, and that was it. It was not a very onerous task. I think it only involved giving three lectures a year at the Incorporated Society's Hall; but that didn't survive the merger, interestingly.

This was after integration, wasn't it?

1957, yes.

No. I have no recollection of that coming up as an issue at the Council when I was there. Much of the Council work was done behind closed doors, and you had to be very lively to get behind what the committee was up to.

I think probably there is still a tendency of that sort, isn't there?

I really don't know how it operates now. It was 1963 when I left - it is now, what, 16 years since I left; it is a long time.

Yes. That is when you became much more interested in economics?

Well, I was determined. I'd been interested all my life, and I was determined to apply some time to it.

Yes. Can I show you something else. I got interested in statements of general accounting principles. I got wondering why it was that the profession, every now and again, comes up with a great sweeping gesture and says: 'We are going to set up a study group to look at the fundamental principles of accounting', which it has done time and time again. It struck me that this must have been a response to some sort of crisis or another. So I set to, to try and find out what sort of crisis that could be.

I can write down the fundamental principles of accounting in five minutes.

[laugh] Yes. If you can write it in 5 minutes you can dictate it in two minutes.

Definition: this is accounting as a science - not accounting as an art but accounting as a science I'm speaking of. Definition: a systematic method of recording transfers of value. All we need now is 1, 2, 3. There is one rule - double entry. It is not a trick of the accountant - this is because a transfer involves a 'come from' and a 'go to'. 'The quality of mercy is not strained; it blesses him that gives and him that receives.'

So there is only one rule. There are only two accounts, fundamentally. There is a 'you' account and there is a 'me' account. And as one's possessions become more extensive, you have to start to separate your wife's from your assets [laugh]. And there are only three jobs: writing, adding - there is multiplication, but that is only a specialised form of addition - and sorting and balancing. Finish. That is the whole science of accounting.

Now science as an art, of course, is something very different, and its complications. It is a language - a mode of investigation. Complications reflect the world in which we live; but as a science, it is something very simple. And if students were taught the simplicity at the beginning

Well, we try to do that.

….. it would help them a lot. Have you tried them on this basis?

Well, we use a book by a chap called [Allan] Barton, an Australian, and we teach them some double entry book keeping right at the very beginning.

Yes. Well have you tried my…?

Not in your formulation.

My 1, 2, 3 framework is very simple and comprehensive.

What I've started to do is to see where we have got initiatives taken, in this country and in America, towards statements of general accounting

principles. There was one set up in America in 1933, for example. They set up a working party to discover the underlying principles of accounting. I found 12 occasions in America and six cases in Britain where an initiative had been taken. And the next question was to find out why - why did they keep going on when nothing ever came out at the end. So I thought well let's have a look at a number of variables. I looked to see whether they were related to increases in the general price level. They didn't appear to be, particularly; there was no great link up there. You had initiatives taken sometimes when prices went down and sometimes when prices went up.

Well, it could be.

Then I had a look at litigation, to see whether it was anything to do with law cases which were cropping up in America. No, nothing was happening there. The law cases had been quite unrelated. Now, the third thing I looked at was quite extraordinary. It was to look at falls in stock market prices year on year. And time after time after time, once there was an initial fall in stock market prices it was followed by an initiative. It came down, and there was a working group set up.

Then in America the same sort of thing happened again. Falls in stock market prices there set off the first initiative; then again another initiative; then again another initiative, all within 12 months. In something like 16 out of the 18 cases [where an initiative was taken], there had been a fall in stock market prices within a year before the initiative was taken. And that is out of only 22 such initial falls [in stock market prices]. It looks to me as though there is some sort of connection there. This is, if you like, looking for something without having a theory to explain it just yet. There does seem to be a link.

Well, that is the better way of looking.

It is a feasible way, yes.

Starting outside, and building it up brick by brick.

Yes. There does seem to be some sort of a connection between falls in stock market prices and then the response by the profession. It is a very general response, to go out and look for the principles of accounting...... it is rather like searching for the Holy Grail. Now - how about having some lunch?

Sir Basil Smallpeice
Interviewed by
Michael Mumford

11ᵗʰ October 1979 at the Atheneum, London

Clearly, to begin at the beginning in terms of your contribution, you qualified in a professional firm?

Yes.

And did you continue in practice after qualifying, or did you go straight into industry?

Not one day. No, I was articled, actually, to a Norwich firm, Bullimore & Co., in 1925. And then they opened a branch office in London in 1926. My parents moved to London at the same time. And the partner who I was articled to was the partner who started Bullimore's London office, and so I moved up with him. Actually, he and I ran the whole practice as it were in London, although I was only a raw articled clerk of about one year's standing. The partner I was articled to was Arnold Kent. But the interesting thing about that was that being in a small firm in London, you get involved in everything. I mean, previously we had been, in the main - at least my experience had been, in the main - with boot and shoe company audits; being in Norwich, you would expect that, with Norwich the centre for ladies' shoes, and Northampton for men's shoes. We moved between the two.

But coming up to London, old Granville Bullimore, who was the founder of the firm, had quite an association with the Curry family, Curry's cycle shops as they were then. Of course, they've grown and grown; but we set up the accounting for the whole of the 100 odd branches around the country. I'm not sure who did the audit: I think we did the audit as well. You can't do that sort of thing now! [laugh]. But that is how it started, and how I came to be in London. And then when I qualified in 1930, or when I was fairly sure that I'd probably passed the Final [examinations], I started looking for a job in industry.

And then I got one as an accountant at Hoover, who were then only importing vacuum cleaners, and they had an office just off Regent Street. But they were about to build a factory, and it was on a ....

... on their present site?

... Yes, and that is why I joined, at Perivale at Western Avenue [London]. The decision hadn't been taken when I went there, although I knew it was in the wind and it was taken soon afterwards. And we bought this land - nine acres at Perivale, and built a factory on it which in the course of the next five years we enlarged. We doubled twice, so it ended up four times the size it was built.

In four years?

Five.

That would be taken us to 1935 or 1936, which was the time that the Accounting Research Association [ARA] was started up; were you in any way connected with the ARA?

No. I don't actually know what you mean by the Accounting Research Association. It wasn't the thing that Ronald Edwards was involved with, was it?

Yes, it was.

Oh, well I used to see Ronald Edwards often through the 1930s, and afterwards of course, yes. Well, I knew Ronald Edwards but I thought he was at the London School of Economics?

He was indeed. Yes. He and Cosmo Gordon set up a Research Association.

Yes.

Together with Mr Eric Hay Davison, who was the original auditor, and Mr Norman Lancaster.

Oh yes, I remember old Lancaster.

And that ran - it is very difficult to put the picture together on that because there is so little published evidence - but it ran until the middle of the war, and then it lost steam. But they did publish a number of papers, and I'm hot on the trail of the published papers.

There were seminars, weren't there, at the London School of Economics?

Yes, there were; but I never went to one until after the war. That was one of Ronnie Edwards's things. In fact, I didn't go to one until the 1950s, I think.

I think they are still going strong. What about the London Industrial Chartered Accountants Group?

Well, actually there is a lot that happened before that; I don't know if it is of interest?

Yes, very much so.

Why would I bother to get involved with that sort of thing? So I think the reason I went into industry, quite frankly, was that I found auditing in itself extremely dull and unproductive, and I didn't see any future in a life in which I would really be checking up what other people had done. When I got to the last few months of my articles, I had firmly made up my mind, having had the advantage of doing productive work - productive accounting work - with Curry's because we were constructing the system for them and incidentally other things as well. I felt that there really must be some more productive corporate function one can put accounting to than just auditing. And so I set out to look for it.

When Hoover started their factory, I got in touch with the American parent company in North Canton, Ohio, and from them I began to learn what standard costing was all about; how you could work accounts from the actual production process and that sort of thing, and then in due course they would themselves become the financial accounts. I thought the view that existed at that sort of date - that cost accounts were one thing and financial accounts were different, and in the end you had to reconcile them - was all so stupid. I began to set it up in Hoover in that sort of way.

Now, Hoover in America already were using standard costing?

Yes, they were already using it, that is right.

And were you aware that they'd been doing it for some time?

They had been doing so for a number of years, that is right.

The developments there seem to have taken place from 1914 to 1920.

Well, as so often, things develop in America ten years before they do here, [laugh] but what the exact number of years was I don't know. But I learnt a lot from - whatever he was called: chief accountant or controller or comptroller of Hoover at North Canton. He used to come over and help me, and gave me their accounting manual and all that sort of thing. And then, which is a thing I've done all my life, having started the thing like that, I then promptly proceeded to get in an assistant to carry it on, because the last thing I wanted to do was to go on doing the thing, having set it up. And I brought in a man from Crosse & Blackwell called George Meads - at least, he was known to everybody as George, although his initials were H.G. and the 'G' stood for Godfrey; but everybody called him George, anyway. And he then came in and became the accountant when I was the chief accountant.

Was he a chartered accountant?

He was a chartered accountant. He ran the thing, and indeed after I left Hoover in 1937 he stayed on and saw it right through until the time came for him to retire. However, while I was still with Hoover, I wanted to find out more - you know, I could see that accounting was an absolutely essential part of the machinery of managing industry. The people that I got into touch with - and I forget how; it was possibly accidental - I went to a thing called the Management Library, in Bloomsbury Square, because I wanted to learn about management and what was done about management, and what there was to be learnt about it. And the

Management Library was run by a person called Esmond Milward, who is still alive today, but not very well. He gave me books to read, and in particular General Motors - I forget what was the name of the president of General Motors …

Sloan?

Sloan: A. P. Sloan, that is right. I learnt a lot from A. P. Sloan's book. And then also E.A. Filene of Boston, a retail firm; I learnt an awful lot from them - a tremendous lot. I never went to see them, but this was merely from the books. And then Esmond Milward put me in touch with the management research groups.

I see. The Management Library itself, was that an independent library?

That was an entirely independent library, run and owned by Esmond Milward: actually, run entirely by Esmond Milward but part financed by Lyn Urwick, of Urwick Orr and Partners, the founder of it. So I said to Esmond: 'I'm terribly interested in management. I'd love to know more about it', and so he put me in touch with management research groups and I caused Hoover to join. I forget which group we were in. I mean, the 'big time people' - the big companies - were in Group 1, but then we were somewhere in [Groups] 2 to 6.

They were ranked by size, were they, rather than main industry?

I'm not sure - size or geography: size for number 1, but the others …? And I went to see through them the operation of Morris Engines at Coventry and I saw that actually in operation. I learnt a tremendous lot. The chap who was the chief accountant there, of Morris Engines, was entirely unqualified except by sheer experience, and he had developed the system of control throughout that factory, and again I learnt an awful lot from him. That was on standard costing lines, but not so fully developed as the Hoover system.

And then another person I learnt an awful lot from was H. A. Simpson, of United Steel Company - Steel, Peach and Tozer, actually. Steel, Peach and Tozer are outside Sheffield. Now, he had been brought in for Steel, Peach and Tozer when it was virtually down and out, and in that situation the workforce had come to learn that their only hope - and the management too - was to stick to the system that he was introducing, because it was their one hope of being financial viable. And he developed that tremendously. I used to go up there several times and just study management, and how accounting worked and contributed to management from that.

Now that was in 1934-6. Now come 1936 we had - I don't know whether this is all boring or not...

No, it is very, very useful, indeed.

Come 1936, the Hoover plant had grown to four times its original size in the space of five years, and I felt that it was high time we had our organisation looked at. So I persuaded the directors. There were only three directors then: Charles Colston, his brother Eric Colston who was the salesman, and Jimmy Wax who was the sort of accountant. I mean, he was a sort of bookkeeper first, but he became a director. I don't think he was qualified either. But I persuaded the three of them to invite Urwick Orr & Partners, and Lyn Urwick himself supervised the assignment, and from then onwards, of course, I've had a very close association with him and his firm. In fact, I shall go and see him again when I'm in Australia at the end of this month, which I always do when I'm in Australia. He put in a report which I thought was quite good as

to how the structure of the company should be reorganised, because it
was then so much bigger.

**The United Kingdom firm was quite independent of the American
firm?**

In terms of management structure, absolutely. We worked within a
budget, of course; we had to submit a budget every year and get approval
- broad approval - of the budget. As long as we didn't fall down on that,
they left us alone.

But it was still much smaller than the American operation?

Oh, much smaller. But the Colstons wouldn't hear of it. So I thought,
well damn this; if they are not going to sort of modernise or bring their
management structure up to date, I think I've had enough here. I've
learnt a lot, and I'd like to get into some completely different sort of
industry - British, rather than American - and just see how things worked
there. Incidentally, during the latter part of this period I was in touch
with Ronny Edwards, and you must talk to him. There is one or two
other of the sort of people who have been young chartered accountants,
and who have been in my years of study. I went to the Metropolitan
College. At least, I took a course at the Metropolitan College at St.
Albans and I came to know a few people, and talked to Ronny Edwards
and that sort of thing. So I started looking round for a job.

**You didn't at that stage come across Lawrence Robson or the Robson
Morrow people, because they were very interested in standard cost
accounting?**

That is right: they were indeed. They were indeed. [laugh] This is
probably libellous but one thing they failed to understand was how to

use it productively. They knew how to work the system, but they didn't know how to use it in management. And this is, I think, one of the great failings of firms of professional accountants in practice, that they've never worked in management, and they don't know how management operates. This was one of the problems I found with Lawrence Robson; he was very interested in it, but he wasn't practical about it.

So I looked round for a job, and I answered an advertisement in *The Times*, and I got what I thought might be a complete change of atmosphere and went to Doulton's. Well, apart from anything else, I wanted something with a number of factories in it, and of course they had six scattered up and down from Kent to Lancashire - St. Helen's through the potteries and that sort of thing.

They covered ceramics and industrial ceramics as well as tableware, didn't they?

Indeed, yes; industrial ceramics. Also, the other thing I said to myself was that I want to stay in London, quite frankly, because one meets so many more people in London, and they've got an office on the Embankment where they still had a pottery working in those days - although it wasn't much good. The last drainpipe pottery had been moved down to Erith in Kent, about in the early 1930s, where what was the Ministry of Works and Buildings now stands. I can't think what it is called now. And so I went there.

Then, soon afterwards of course, the war started and so on. But, again, I was fascinated because, going up to say Burslem, and seeing the fine china works up there, they employed 1500 people at their works. And they hadn't any idea of what was going on in the place and how to control it. The potteries were extremely short of clerical labour because nobody ever thought it necessary to employ any, but however I rooted out an accountant from one of the local firms of auditors called Harold Shipley - that was the chap I rooted out. And he came and joined me, and we started introducing modern accounting in this fine china place at Burslem.

I suppose one of the problems would be that clerical labour is very often women, and they are all employed in ……

They were all employed in the pottery, yes that is right. But, equally, I think management hadn't realised; I mean, they merely kept debtors' ledgers and they kept order books, and that sort of thing, but otherwise, [laugh] they had very little control. But it was very interesting. And then the war came, and the managing director, who was a Lieutenant Commander Green, came from Price Waterhouse, but he wasn't qualified. After retiring from the navy, he went into Price Waterhouse because he felt he could learn something about how financial control of business could be exercised. And old Nicholas Waterhouse was the auditor of Doulton's. And shortly before I started looking for a job, Basil Green had been taken into Doulton's on Nicholas Waterhouse's advice, because he could see that the whole Doulton business was so slackly controlled, financially. And he persuaded the then chairman, Eric Hooper, who was a Doulton, his mother having been a Doulton; he persuaded him to take Basil Green in. And then Basil Green started looking round for somebody to come and really look after the financial side, which is how he persuaded the then chairman, Eric Hooper, to let me come in.

Then I was fairly occupied. He went off as soon as he was called up after Munich, because he was RNR [in the Royal Naval Reserve]. Then he came back to us. Then, as soon as war - or just before war - broke out, he was called up again, and I found myself in a position of being acting managing director, unpaid [laugh] - I mean unpaid for that function. I remained there throughout the war except for the period when I went into the Treasury, but we will leave that on one side. It was during the beginning of the war that I really started, because being in a reserved occupation I was full of energy which, in a war time situation, I couldn't really use.

And so I got together with one or two chartered accountants, like myself, who were similarly reserved, and we thought, look, we have got to do something about this stupid profession of ours, which is so tied down to just auditing and a bit of tax. And I got together a group. Now, I can't place the date of it, but one of the chaps in it was a fellow called Castells who was in Glaxo.

What was his name?

Castells. He later had cancer, I think, and he faded out of the scene, but he was one. I can't remember who else was in the group. I remember Harry Norris was there. Perhaps not at that stage, because he was too young.

I hope to see him.

Yes, but I can't remember. We had a group of about six, and I wrote papers as a basis of discussion; we used to meet in the Doulton offices of an evening, and every now and then air raid sounds would go and all that sort of thing. But the result of our deliberations - I wrote it entirely myself, and Castells did a certain amount of editing of it - but it was published in *The Accountant* anonymously by 'A Group of Accountants in Industry': that was all it was described as, and it was called 'The Future of Auditing'. I'm not sure whether I've even got a copy of it now.

Well, if it is in *The Accountant*, it can be traced.

Yes. Well, that would be, I would say, early 1941 because apart from anything else I met Castells in the Treasury. I only stayed in the Treasury for ten weeks, I think. I was persuaded to go into the Treasury by Lyn Urwick, who had gone into the Treasury to set up an Organisation and Methods Department. This was in 1940, and he persuaded me to go in, and old Reggie Wilson - Sir Reginald Wilson - he was one of them that was there. Castells was another, I was another; there were a few of us. But Reggie Wilson didn't become a member of my little group, actually; he stayed on at the Treasury. But I left the Treasury after ten weeks. I was so disgusted with the stupid things that went on in terms of paper systems, and I thought to hell with this: I'm much more use back in Doulton's, where at least we are in the industrial ceramics industry and making things for the war effort.

Perhaps it was a stroke of bad luck that you weren't involved with the Ministry of Production.

Well, it might have been.

Where de Paula and people were trying to get things made.

That is right, yes. Well, now, the publication of this leaflet on the future of auditing triggered off quite a furore. And I think it must have been the next Annual General Meeting of the Institute, there was so many people turned up at it in Moorgate Place … I mean, people were queuing to get into the building, let alone to get into the room. Old Charles Palmour, who was then he was then senior partner of Whinney Smith & Whinney, was President of the Institute for four years, because they didn't change once the war got really under way. I don't think he knew what hit him [laugh]. But at any rate they had to adjourn the meeting without starting it. But I suppose this was a feeling, you know - it had triggered off a feeling within the practising side, as well as alerting people who were not in it, but were in industry.

Yes. But none of this comes through the official records, of course. There is just a reference to the 1941 Annual General Meeting.

1941 Annual General Meeting; well, I was right yes. Well, that is right, and it was adjourned, and then it was reopened in the room that I think was previously the ice rink at Grosvenor House. There was a terrific crowd - I don't know how many thousand people turned up, but there were one or two, I suppose, which is unusual for an Annual General Meeting of the Institute [laugh]. And it was following that that a thing was started called the Taxation and Financial Relations Committee.

That was set up at that stage, and I was asked to become a member of it, but the thought of anybody in industry ever being on the Council of the Institute - I mean, it was just completely unheard of - unthinkable [laugh]. And so they set up this committee, on which it was legitimate that people from outside the pale could come into the Institute premises: you know, that sort of thing.

You were not able to become a Fellow of course, were you; you were an Associate?

Oh, Lord no, not for many years [laugh]. Frederick de Paula, who was chief accountant of Dunlop, he was one of the first industrial members of it; and Percy Rees, who was chief accountant at Unilever, he was there; and I was there. There was a chap from Hudson's Bay Company; I can't think what his name would be. Robinson, I think. and I can't remember who else, but at any rate this ......

Did you know these people already; did you know Rees and de Paula?

Oh, I knew Freddie de Paula, yes, and Percy Rees. You know, I'd heard about them. Well, actually one of the interesting things was that Esmond Milward, who ran the Management Library, ran a series of what were called Milward's Dinners, at which people in industry would get together and talk about problems. We used to meet at Oldenino's in Lower Regent Street. And I met quite a number of people there. I may have met Freddy de Paula there - I can't remember now.

Well he was also very much involved with LSE, wasn't he?

Probably, probably through Ronald Edwards; I can't remember. At any rate, that doesn't matter all that much how I got to know them, but I did. And then, it must have been fairly soon after this, that I broke through another barrier because I was the first non-practising member of the London Committee of Chartered Accountants.

The London District Society.

Well, it wasn't a District Society in those days. District Societies were for the provinces. [laugh] London - no, you couldn't have a District Society in London. So it was the London Society of Chartered Accountants. And then I started agitating in the London Society Committee. A chap who was always very sympathetic to me this time was Wynne Bankes, who was the secretary of the Institute in those days; he was all for a little bit of internal revolution [laugh], and Alan MacIver who succeeded him.

But I then started agitating to get what I call an industrial chartered accountant on the Council. Then, of course, only Fellows of the Institute could be members of the Council. I forget who I talked to on the Council; certainly Charles Palmour, who wasn't very receptive. But there were other senior members. There was a man called Shepherd who practised down in Cardiff, who subsequently became president one year. And, of course Barton, of Barton Mayhew. I used to talk to him and he was very sympathetic, very. And I can't remember the date, but I eventually persuaded them that they'd got to let some industrial chartered accountants in. All right, they'd got to be Fellows. I then set to work on Percy Rees, and he wouldn't - at first [laugh]. So I then switched my attention to Frederick de Paula, and he said yes - he would. So I then went …..

But then, he was also in practice, of course, wasn't he; he wasn't purely in industry?

He was not in practice at the time. He gave up the practice when he went to Dunlop. Now Percy Rees had been in practice, and he gave up practice when he went to Unilever, or Lever Brothers as it was in those days. They gave up their practice when they went. But they were both FCAs, because they'd been in practice. And so I said: 'You know, if you two don't take this on, we will never get anywhere'. And so they were duly elected, put up by the London Committee. They were duly elected. I forget what year that was, but that would certainly be on the records.

That is 1942 or 1943, yes.

1942, I should think, yes. It was soon after I went on the London Committee, which was in 1942. And then - it must have been about that time that I got together with Eric Hay Davison and one or two others, and we decided to start a lunch group of industrial chartered accountants. And he and I decided this at lunch in the Holborn Restaurant, and it started from that.

In 1942, probably?

I should think so. I forget who was the third member of the lunch; it might have even been Ronnie Edwards, but he wouldn't have been part of the group. So Eric Davison and I started this, and we used to meet. We had our lunches in a private room on the first floor of Antoine's Restaurant, as it was in those days, in Charlotte Street, and we used to meet once a month. There was a chap who was from Bryant and Mays who came along fairly early, and - oh yes - somebody from Harrods. He was then the accountant of Harrods; George Myers. Yes, so you know, we were gradually spreading the net wider. I don't think Harry Norris came at that stage; he came a little bit later.

What about Fea - W. W. Fea; was he?

Bill Fea was, certainly, of GKN. That is right. And he was one of the early ones. I'm not sure that he wasn't the third person at this lunch.

Well, I also hope to see him in a month or so.

Yes, well he would be able to confirm or deny that. But we started these lunches, and I was the person who organised them and my office did the invitations and that sort of thing. And we achieved something because we got Wynne Bankes to bring the President of the Institute along!

Good Lord.

And yes [laugh] and soon afterwards at the Annual General Meeting in 1943 or 1944 they amended the rules so that ACAs could become members of the Council. ['ACA' refers to Associate members of the Institute, in contrast to FCAs or Fellows.] And I was elected in 1940 - oh, maybe it was a bit later, I can't remember the date but you will be able to check it up. I was the first ACA ever to go on the Council. There is no distinction at the moment: under the modern rules, I would have been an FCA long ago. But I was the first really industrial accountant - chartered accountant - ever to go on the Council. And Jack Clayton came along soon after or maybe at the same time and Bill Fea; there were five of us: de Paula, Rees, me, Jack Clayton and Bill Fea.

That is how we breached the defences [laugh]. Of course, by then I suppose they'd come to see that people like de Paula and Rees were not all that bad, and they thought: 'well, we had better let the ACAs in'. This was quite a revolution in the Institute.

It must have become evident, too, by that time or just about that time that there was a majority of members who were not in practice - or who did not engage as partners in practice.

That is right. But they didn't care a damn about ACAs in practice - the ACAs on the practising side. But they were made to care about the ACAs in industry. And from that, a lot followed.

I didn't go on the Council in 1948 - I've got the dates wrong. I went through the chair of the London Committee first, so it didn't happen as quickly as I've suggested. And I think probably the president of the Institute who came along to lunch and whom we converted was not Palmour. It must have been the next president. It might well have been Gilbert Shepherd or Harold Howitt.

[reading the History of the ICAEW] Harold Barton was 1944/45.

Harold Barton, 1944/45?

Yes, and then Howitt in 1945/46, and then Jones, and then Shepherd in 47/48.

It was Harold Howitt, I'm pretty sure, who came along and whom we converted. And therefore that puts the date of the changing of the rules back to about 1946, because Harold Howitt would have carried it through. So correct my earlier dates on that!

Right.

But by then, of course, this London - I don't know what we called it, London Lunch Group - was growing quite a lot. I mean we'd got numbers who regularly came along of about 12 or 15 or so.

There wouldn't be anywhere a list of the speakers who came to these lunches, would there?

I don't think we had speakers to begin with. We just met and talked about whatever happened to come into our minds. No, we didn't have organised speakers.

Was Bray - F. Sewell Bray - involved at all?

Yes. I think that was a completely different line. Somehow or other I got involved with youth work; I can't think how on earth I got involved. And there was a chap who was deputy chairman he was a noble lord. Barbara Ward was involved and Sam Courtauld was very interested in this group. He used to invite me regularly and George Gouder, of the Ministry of Supply. Barbara Ward was at that time writing of course for *The Economist* and I forget - one or two others. No I think that was about the group. We used to have dinner at the Connaught where he [Courtauld] had a very nice cellar accumulated before the war [laugh].

And then we used to go round to his house at 12 North Audley Street and talk about this, that or the other. And, of course, this strengthened also my relations with Eric Davison who was in Courtaulds. I used to see a lot of Sam Courtauld. I think he was a wonderful person. I learnt a lot from him, too, about management of people in industry. It is surprising; one wouldn't have thought it, but he knew how to handle people. He knew how to get loyalty out of them: very impressive.

Was there any sort of connection with the Department of Applied Economics at Cambridge?

None that I'm aware of.

What I have in my mind is the institution of the National Institute of Economics and Social Research, which was about 1938, and Stone - Richard Stone - because he and Sewell Bray knew each other very well. Bray was later a senior research fellow at Cambridge. I just wondered how that came about. It wasn't through this group?

No, it wasn't through that group. But at any rate that is how it went on.

After the war ended I felt that I badly needed to get somebody into Doulton's to really get the accounting and financial control side going. And then I recruited a person called Ken Bevan whom I suggest you should go and see. He had been in an ordinance factory near Manchester. What is the university near Manchester? Salford.

Salford, yes; there was an ordnance factory at Salford.

Well, I think he was running that. And, incidentally, so was Henry Benson who was involved in that from the outside; Ken Bevan was on the inside. Anyway, Ken Bevan came and joined me. As you will have gathered, I am fond of getting other people to do the work, and he took on the construction of the accounting control side of Doulton.

However, we were getting nowhere in terms of developing the business. Basil Green had come back from the war; he had been a regional commissioner or deputy regional commissioner in the South East, and he came back to us and took on being managing director again. We were getting absolutely nowhere, because of the old chairman who really regarded his function like that of a lord of a manor with tenants; we were the people who ran the different factories. But he didn't want the thing to grow; he didn't want to get any bigger at all.

Sounds very familiar from the Potteries.

That is right. At any rate, I just wanted to go on the board and Basil Green was receptive. Peter Doulton, who was a nephew of the chairman and was in the business, came back after the war. He wanted to go on the board but his uncle Eric Hooper wouldn't have it, so he left and went elsewhere and built up a wonderful business - much better than he would ever have done in his uncle's firm. And when I was told that they wouldn't have anybody inside on the board other than the managing director, I decided to pack it in.

I'll tell you who was another person who was in this lunch group of ours from the very beginning of this lunch group, and that is Joseph Latham, from the National Coal Board. He was with Manchester Collieries and then National Coal Board. He was one of the first industrial members on the Council, Joseph Latham. I met him quite by accident on holiday in the Lake District during the war. We both were walking the fells or something, and I found he was there, from Manchester Collieries, and then, after the war when the National Coal Board was set up, he appeared there. I was talking to him about my disillusionment with Doulton's and how we couldn't just get anywhere at all. And he said: 'why don't you come to me? I'd be glad of assistance.' And I thought, well that is too close quarters; we were too much of an age anyway.

And then I went to talk to Reggie Wilson about it, who had by then become comptroller of the British Transport Commission. And he said: 'Well come to me because I badly need somebody'. He got me to parade before Sir Cyril Hurcombe, as he was in those days, who was the chairman of the British Transport Commission. And I went to him at the Transport Commission at Broadway in Westminster in 1948 as Director of Costs and Statistics. There was so much to be done there, but it was so vast. I think there were something like 600,000 employees.

Good gracious.

And way up in the ivory tower, at 65 Broadway, you know, one couldn't get near the people who were doing the job. Now this has always seemed to me to be an absolute essential of the operation of the financial control. In a business, you must be near the people who are doing the job, and get them to have confidence in what you are trying to do and understand what they're trying to do. And whether it is airline pilots or whatever it is, that rule applies. You've got to get alongside them, and they've got to understand the way your mind works, and you've got to learn how their minds work.

And so after a year I thought this is hopeless; I don't think this commission is ever going to get anywhere. And Cyril Hurcombe was of course a civil servant of long standing and great seniority, and he hadn't got any ideas either about making things grow or humanising them. I mean, he was essentially an administrator, and so I packed it in.

I was then on the Council of the Institute. I joined the Council of the Institute in 1948, and I decided in 1949 to pack this in [work at the British Transport Commission], and I went to see Harold Howitt, who had become a great friend of mine, a personal friend. And curiously enough - these are how these coincidences work in life - he said: 'Well, it is amazing you've come to see me today. I've only this morning been to see Sir Miles Thomas, who is the new chairman of British Overseas Airways Corporation [BOAC], and he has asked me to find somebody to come in and put financial control in throughout BOAC'.

Extraordinary; not only that, but you had come from the transport industry.

Well, of course, that helped the matter, obviously. Harold Howitt had been on the Air Council in the war, and he had been on the board of BOAC when it was set up in 1946. And for a period he had stood in as temporary chairman, before Harold Hartley had gone there.

I didn't know that.

And Miles Thomas had known him from that. Of course, Miles Thomas was brought in by Harold Hartley, as a member of the board but nothing more in the first place. So it was natural when Miles Thomas was looking round for somebody in charge of the accounts or something for him to go and see Harold, or to ask Harold Howitt to go and see him.

I went to see Miles Thomas and liked him from the word go. But I walked round and round Green Park because BOAC's offices were then just on Piccadilly. And I decided to turn it down because I thought: 'no, I'd had enough of nationalised industries, thank you very much, from my experience in the Transport Commission'. And so I said: 'no, I'm sorry but I don't think I can take it'. And at the next Council meeting a month later, Harold Howitt said to me: 'You know, I'm sorry you turned that job down. You ought not to have done that, because there is a tremendous lot to be done there, and you will find working with Miles Thomas very different from anything in the Transport Commission'. He said: 'to begin with, it is much smaller; they've only got about 20,000 people there, compared with 600,000'.

I began to think, well maybe there is something in this. And he said: 'I wish you'd go and see Miles again'. So I said: 'oh, all right - I will'. And I went and I fell for it. So that is how it happened. Cyril Hurcombe didn't exactly like my leaving the Transport Commission, but he couldn't stop me. And so on the 1st of January 1950 I started with BOAC. Miles Thomas wanted me to be financial controller, but I said: 'No, you've got this wrong; if a finance man thinks his going to control everybody, then you've got the wrong man. But I don't mind taking the American title of comptroller, because comptrolling is not controlling what other people do. It is counting and comparing and providing them with the information to enable them to do their own controlling. And he said: 'well, I take your point; but I must have the word 'financial' in it'. So we compromised on 'financial comptroller' [laugh], so that is how that stupid title came about. And then it flowed from that.

The British Overseas Airways Corporation had already been in operation for some time by then, had they?

For four years. No - sorry, that is not right. It had been set up by the Conservatives as a public corporation in 1939, and Sir John Reith, who had up till then been Director General of BBC, was asked to become its first chairman, and took it on in 1939. Then, when the war finally hotted up in 1940, he went across to the Ministry of War Transport

I asked simply whether there was an earlier corporation because I was under the impression - I wasn't certain - that it was not one of the post war nationalised industries.

No, it was set up by the Conservatives as a public corporation and John Reith was the first chairman. I came to know John Reith well in later years, but not until I got to BOAC. He was most helpful. Of course, when the Labour Government in 1946 started setting up nationalised industries, there was a ready made public corporation and it was just too easy to change the label to 'Nationalised Industry'. And John Reith always regretted so much that the concept of a public corporation, which had been developed within the BBC and then began to be applied to BOAC, was then taken away from it.

Yes. Was it reporting within the Companies Acts; was it filing accounts?

What - the public corporation?

BOAC, specifically.

Well, during the war it was on government account, so I don't know if they put the accounts into the Treasury. God knows what happened to them. But, I mean, nobody worried about cost in the war - and that is where a lot of the trouble started.

I wasn't quite sure whether it was publishing its accounts.

Oh yes, from 1946 - from the word go, when it was nationalised. And there was a system of government grants to cover deficits through for ten years. And, of course, Miles Thomas did what he did, and helped a little by me I hope, we were able to get out of any government grant in six years, instead of ten. And BEA went on for the full ten [years], but they never like to admit it! [laugh].

Did you maintain your connections with the luncheon club over the whole of this period? The luncheon club went on for some years, didn't it?

Oh yes. Well, then it became made much more respectable by calling itself 'The London Industrial Chartered Accountants' Group' - LICAG. I gave up after joining and starting with BOAC. I gave up and again left it to others to carry on, because I was so busy. But Ken Bevan went on going to it fairly regularly, and he maintained the contacts and kept in touch. But I used to go along once or twice a year, that is all, for many years.

Were you involved at all with the refresher courses in 1946?

Was I not? Yes, I got led into that somehow or other, I can't tell you how. But I remember going down to Cambridge, and I met various people who told me they are indebted to me for things that I said which I can't now remember. But I taught then about the uses of accounting in management.

That seems to have been a very, very important institution, again. People met, and there was such enthusiasm and interest.

Yes, that is right. And also I seem to remember going down to 'The House' [Christ Church College] at Oxford, too.

Yes. There were one or two innovations within the Institute at the end of the war. There was a committee or a sub committee which looked at mechanised accounting.

Yes, there was.

But you weren't involved yourself in that?

No - well, I can't remember. I was, but by 1950 I was so involved in BOAC and setting up proper financial controls because they'd never got out of this period of government accounting during the war. And so I just hadn't got the time for anything after 1950. I do remember being involved in something by Freddie de Paula that he wanted me to check through - some paper about cost accounting or something like that.

That sounds right; that sounds as though it would have come at about that time.

Yes, but then you see I desperately needed somebody to do the donkey work of working out the system and implementing it in BOAC, although we were cutting down. Miles Thomas did a fantastic job. He cut the staff down by one third from 24,000. It was 24,000 by the time British South American Airways [BSAA] had been brought into it - because when the Tudors [aircraft] fell into the Atlantic, British South American Airways went out of business.

I'm sorry; I don't understand the statement 'the Tudors fell into the Atlantic'.

Well, they disappeared into the Caribbean part of the Atlantic, carrying full loads of passengers.

Good Lord.

This was in the late 1940s - 1948 or 1949.

It was a new plane was it?

The Avro Tudor.

Yes; this was a newly developed plane?

Converted bombers. Two of them disappeared. Nothing was ever found of them, or their crew or passengers.

Was this in this mysterious 'Bermuda Triangle'?

Yes. It was near there. But, obviously, the plane wasn't airworthy, and so BSAA went out of business. BOAC were asked to take them on, and we took all their staff on. That was, it was 24,000 in 1948 and by 1950, when I joined, it had gone down to about 20,000 and over the next two years Miles Thomas got it down, with a bit of help from me, to just over 16,000. We shed 8,000 without a strike because we told the trade unions what we were doing, told the shop stewards what we were doing, we told them everything, explained why - and we got it down without a strike.

I'm sorry to interrupt again, but I was going to go back a little bit. Talking about 1948, were you involved with the FBI?

Yes, I was.

At that stage, the FBI was campaigning very hard, wasn't it, on this matter of inflation accounting and the burden of taxation?

Well, to be absolutely frank with you, I had not heard the words 'inflation accounting' at that date - in 1948, I hadn't any idea at all. But I was involved with the FBI because Eric Hooper was chairman of Doulton's and so as head of a business in the London area was a member of its 300-man council or whatever it was. And also, one of the people whom he brought onto the board of Doulton's was Sir Guy Locock, who was the previous director of the FBI before Norman Kipping. Eric Hooper asked me to take an interest in - I don't know, some accounting matter - and Guy Locock also nudged my arm and said 'go and see what you can do'. [laugh]

Yes. Jack Clayton was very important there, wasn't he?

Yes. Of course, I got to know Jack Clayton quite a lot through this group, this lunch group. But when I wanted somebody to come into BOAC, of course I knew the person I wanted and that was Ken Bevan, whom I'd left behind in Doulton's. I went to see Basil Green, the managing director of Doulton's, and Barry Hooper the chairman and said: 'look this chap is just the chap I want; do you mind if I pinch him from you?' And Ken Bevan was only too delighted to be asked to come, and he came with their full agreement I'm glad to say.

I can't imagine they were terribly happy about that.

Well, they weren't so enthusiastic about modern accounting, quite frankly. And so they let him go without difficulty. I suppose they felt they could get somebody else. But Ken Bevan did a tremendous job in BOAC. And we introduced modern management accounting methods into airline operations before ever the Americans did. Interestingly, the most progressive of the American airlines in terms of financial control was American Airlines, a domestic carrier, and United Airlines who had a public accountant as its president. Pan Am weren't so hot, but we were able to teach them quite a lot, and certainly American Airlines and Pan American both learnt an awful lot from the work that Ken Bevan and I had done. I then became the sort of leader of the financial committee within the International Air Transport Association [IATA]. I wasn't interested in the finances of IATA, but I was interested in the financial control of airlines.

It was quite a good group, actually which I think did the industry quite a bit of good - curiously enough, even Air France. I say 'curiously enough', because they have this habit of having what they call 'inspecteurs' or something: 'inspecteur general' or 'inspecteur de finance' - they're civil servants. The civil service in France is far more powerful than it is in England - or was; they put these people into their publicly owned industries, and he was very interested in what we were doing. So were the Belgians, too. Germans, of course, didn't have an airline at that stage. The Dutch were very good - KLM - first class! I forget the name of the financial controller there whom I used to work very closely with; he came to them from Philips NV.

Oh he did, did he? And the Swiss did they take any part?

Yes, but not awfully much. Walter Bergtold was the person from Swiss Air in those days; he was quite interested. They were a jolly good airline. So really I think it is not unreasonable to claim that the work that Ken Bevan and I did at the beginning of the '50s gradually spread through quite a lot of airlines. We learnt from them, equally, so it wasn't all one way, not by any means. [laugh].

And then you stayed with BOAC for some years, didn't you?

Fourteen years. Then I became managing director in 1956, and I was managing director for eight years up to the end of 1963. But then that is outside your terms of reference [laugh]. It is also outside your period.

Not outside my interests!

Oh yes, but outside your period too, isn't it?

Yes, at the moment. Did you get involved at all with The 1949 Group which had evening meetings? Kenneth Wright was involved in that.

No, I didn't. You see, I was probably fading out a bit at that time. I used to attend. While I was at Doulton's, of course, or in the Transport Commission I was on the Examination Committee of the Institute and I used to set examination papers with Percy Rees of Unilever, and had this terrible job of correcting them - that is a terrible chore. But of course there were only about 1400 people sitting in those days, and not the enormous throng that sits now. But then Percy Rees continued on his own, after I joined BOAC in 1950. I dropped everything. Except I used to go along to committee meetings at the Institute, and Council meetings.

You stayed on the Council for some years?

Oh, yes. Then, finally, after I became managing director of BOAC in 1956, then in 1957 I gave it up.

Were there any particular things which you were anxious, as one of these very early non-practising members of Council, to pursue? Were there respects in which you thought the English Institute needed to be nudged into new initiatives, or new directions?

No, not particularly because I felt that there was so many of us going into industry now. And, you know, they're members of the Institute - by and large, they're the more effective members of the Institute in terms of running the national economy. They all get on and do things their own way. No, I've never ever thought that I was claiming a monopoly of thought in this I field. It is far better to have a great variety of people, tackling many different problems, and they'll find their own solutions. But the one thing I just couldn't abide was keeping records just for the sake of keeping records. Records aren't worth keeping unless they can be put to productive use.

The Institute was doing a lot of work behind the scenes towards the 1948 Companies Act.

Yes, that is right. Well, I would have heard it on the side, and particularly in the T&FR Committee, of which I was a member.

Were you involved with - I nearly said 'the infamous' - N12 on inflation accounting, the price level statement?

I've never been involved. When was it?

It was 1949, N12.

Was it? I don't think I was. In fact, as I said earlier, I didn't recall the phrase inflation accounting, because I didn't realise we had inflation in those days. What was it? About 3% - 4%?

Oh, I think it had reached a dizzy height - I think it was 7.9%.

Only temporarily, because it came down again afterwards.

It came back down again. In the 1950s, it was remarkably constant.

That is right.

But it had reached a peak. I published an article in *Accounting and Business Research* just recently, looking at the debate on inflation accounting between 1948 and 1954 as compared with the debate there has been in the 1970s. There are very, very close similarities between debates in each case, having been initiated by this burst of inflation and a fall in stock prices. Anyway, N12 was a very strong commitment to historical cost, and there was quite a row over this.

Well, historical cost is about the only form of accounting over which you can exert discipline. Once you don't exert discipline, then published accounts can be trimmed to mean almost anything. This is one of the tragedies of the present situation, I think, and I personally feel a good deal of sympathy for people who feel that one wants to stop talking about accounting for profit and talk about accounting for creation of wealth or adding value. There is someone in Leicester - doesn't he advocate all that sort of thing? Well, we all have value added taxes, but I mean unless people create wealth in the sense of producing something that people want at the price you offer it at, you are not really creating anything. Accounting is a bit at sea at the moment.

Who were the leading figures in the T&FR? You mentioned that de Paula was there.

de Paula, Rees - good gracious.

I threw it completely out of the air because it was interesting to see just who struck you.

I've forgotten the names. Lawrence Robson was there, of course - very much so.

Do you ever come across one of Rees's colleagues, a chap called Kenneth Lacey?

No.

He wrote a couple of papers and a book.

Ian Morrow, of course, I've seen quite a lot of over the years, but not latterly.

Yes, I'd like to find out more about those two. I think Mr Rees is no longer with us.

No, he is not. He died some years ago.

What about Carrington; was William Carrington a member of T&FR?

Oh, very much so; he was certainly, yes. Now, since you ask for names, Carrington was indeed - but very much on the taxation side, and Lawson.

Yes, Bill Lawson.

Binder Hamlyn - would that be right?

Thomas Robson - he was another active member of the T&FR.

W. E. Parker?

Oh, W. E. Parker yes. Again, very much on the taxation end of things and not the other. Russell Kettle, curiously enough.

Of Deloittes?

Deloittes. Russell Kettle. There was another one from Deloittes; now, what was his name? We owe a lot to people who contributed at that time. And once we got our foot in the door - when I say 'we,' I mean the people who went into industry without ever having gone into practice - once we got our foot in the door, I think we were quite welcome. It wasn't a rough revolution, in any sense.

There was another aspect of Doulton's I'd like to go back and ask about, and that was the practise of consolidated accounts. Were you consolidating your accounts before the 1947 Companies Act?

No, we didn't have any subsidiary companies. We just had separate works, that is all, at that stage.

That is another interesting story, the origins of consolidation.

That is right, absolutely. Well, I didn't ever get involved personally in that until I went to Cunard, because I mean there is no question of consolidation in BOAC.

Nor with Hoover, because they were unitary.

That is right. But with Cunard, of course, yes - very much so.

Going a little after the time with which I am specifically concerned at the moment, were you involved with Takeover Commission in its earliest forms?

Well, in the early days, Humphrey Mynors was there. Humphrey Mynors I got to know well in the 1940s, along with this Barbara Ward whom I was talking about. But no, I didn't really get involved with it [the Takeover Commission]: I didn't have any cause to.

Were Doulton's a quoted company?

Oh yes, but I left them before that thing was ever set up.

I'd like to find out how the idea of consolidation got under way here because there are a number of different possible routes. You mentioned earlier that the Americans tend to be ten years ahead in a number of ways; they were doing consolidations from 1900 or very shortly after - 1904, 1907. The practice didn't catch on here; I believe that ICI consolidated in 1922, but Dunlop's are generally credited under de Paula, in 1932 and 1933.

Well, look at Unilever. I mean in the days when I used to go round and see Percy Rees, down in Blackfriar's House, to talk about things, in those days they would have had over 300 companies. And of course the de Paula's and the Rees's went into industry for that reason, not to introduce management accounting. And neither of those two - and I'm not denigrating them in any way by saying this - but they didn't know how to use accounts to improve the efficiency of production or distribution and that sort of thing. They were essentially consolidators.

Yes. I gather there was a rather special reason for de Paula being invited into Dunlop's, because Dunlop's had got into something of a tangle and they needed somebody who was quite independent and far beyond any question of doubt.

I dare say. That is right.

And I suppose the point you have just made makes a contrast between those two and Ronnie Edwards, who was very interested in measures of efficiency.

Yes, he was; that is right - certainly so.

Do you know whether he had a commercial background?

No, he didn't.

He got involved during the war in the Electricity Council.

I believe so.

And then he went onto Beechams; he actually became chairman of Beechams.

Some time afterwards, yes.

But I've heard, rather indirectly, that his view of accounting was somewhat soured, and he was told while he was teaching at LSE that he shouldn't be teaching all this management economics - it is debits and credits that are at the heart of the game.

Well, he encouraged me a lot. I mean, he was a stimulating person to talk to. This is one of the great things about meeting and talking to other people; you stimulate each other - or you can do.

Well now how are you going?

Very well indeed. I'll just run down my list of things. [Reading notes] 'District Society'; well, it wasn't the London District Society, it was the 'London Society'. Would they have had a yearly conference or a meeting of some sort? Didn't they have a series of annual weekends?

They had a yearly meeting in the Institute in Moorgate Place in those days, and I addressed it at some stage, I remember. I think Bill Carrington was probably in the chair, or somebody like that at that time.

Well, those records appear in *The Accountant*. I've never asked anyone, but a question came up in my mind as to how *The Accountant* managed to be so well briefed on the affairs of the Institute. Were they allowed to send a report along to meetings?

To meetings of the Institute; do you mean general meetings?

Well, Council meetings.

Well, I don't know. Now, I would have thought they were, and when we had a discussion paper produced by somebody at a meeting, they would have been given a copy of it. They probably had a representative there. But there was a woman who was editor of *The Accountant* at that stage in the 1940s, and she was very good, I thought. I mean one never had the slightest difficulty in getting anything into *The Accountant* if there was anything interesting to say. What on earth was her name? I used to go and have lunch with her at the Cowdray Club which was the ladies' club in those days.

Yes. I don't know the names of the editors of *The Accountant*. It is a curious institution.

What was your view on integration with The Society (the Society of Incorporated Accountants and Auditors)?

Oh, I was for it all the time. Yes, I got involved in that while on the Council.

On the grounds that there were economies of scale to be achieved, and they had a strong non-practising wing - or what?

[laugh] I'm just trying to think why. I mean, it seemed to me a natural thing to do, quite frankly, and I thought it weakened the profession to have two bodies basically all doing auditing and that sort of thing.

Well, my warmest thanks for all the time you have given me.

BRUCE SUTHERLAND

INTERVIEWED BY

MICHAEL MUMFORD

16th November 1979 at
The Institute of Directors, London

I am interested to see what has happened in the past, and to try to identify what causes influenced practice - and, similarly, what causes operated on theory: why some theories catch on and others don't. That is a parallel question. I think there is little doubt that practice is not predicated upon theory; practice is there first, whereas, to some extent, theory tends to follow after practice to explain what is going on. The problems which theorists are interested in explaining arise out of that.

There is a particular area that I wanted to ask you about and that was The 1949 Group.

I was never associated with The 1949 Group.

Right. What about the lunch group which was also formed in the late 1940s - were you associated with that?

Again, I was not associated with that. I mean, I knew of it, but you see I was never in London, and these tended to be London based.

Right. Then the next area was integration.

Let's turn back for a minute to your theory thing. You see, I don't pretend to be anything of an authority on the techniques or whatever of accounting. I've got a Pegler Prize for book-keeping and that sort of thing when I was passing my exams, so I had to know something about it. But, as you probably know, I am today basically a tax man and a manager. I am a mixture: I'm concerned with the management of companies, but I'm also a tax man. But the actual business of preparing accounts - I'm not involved with at all.

I'm involved with the use of accounts a very great deal, obviously, because in my practice I'm probably a leading practitioner on the valuation of unquoted shares, so by definition I'm using accounts there. Also, of course, as I've been the chairman of a public company and I sit on the boards of a number of companies, I'm also interested in the reporting function. However, I wouldn't pretend to be an expert in the techniques. The thing I feel has gone wrong is that people are trying to import more into this than there really is. Basically, what are we doing? Accounts are a means of conveying information, so you are presenting facts - certain facts in a certain form - to people, and the big problem that is bedevilling us at the moment is the fact that we are no longer using a constant yardstick. As Mrs Thatcher said the other day: 'It is time we restored to money its function as a store of value as well as being a medium of exchange'. She is absolutely right.

There are enormous struggles to try and make something meaningful. For my money, I believe that those involved are like Roger Bacon and others who were looking for the 'Philosopher's Stone'. I don't think there is an answer to this one. It is just 30 years ago, in fact, that the old Taxation and Financial Relations Committee of the Institute - the sub committee chaired by Bill Fea - produced the first recommendation ever on the question of the fall in the value of money.

N12, in 1949?

Yes, N12. It is exactly 30 years. And Bill Fea was the chairman of the committee.

I went to see him three weeks ago.

When that came up, I was indignant. I said that they had sat on the fence so long that they might have done better than that. Now, 30 years on, I've come to the conclusion that there isn't a meaningful solution. There have been periods of inflation even wilder than this in the past which have disappeared and turned into periods of deflation, so I could say it is a temporary problem although it may last for a long time as a temporary problem, but people don't understand this. And there is all this effort being made - and strait jackets being made - to force members of the profession to produce accounts in particular ways, regardless of the circumstances of the companies and the events which they are reporting. In other words, they are saying: 'You must report in this form. Forget about the fact that no two companies are the same; somehow, you've got to fit into this strait jacket'.

It arises in part, I think, from the fact that in the period from the end of the war through until after the 1968 integration proposals, we did nothing about raising our entry standards. One of the things I said in the debates on the integration campaign was that apparently the Council of the Institute had never heard of the 1944 Education Act. They just assumed that the General Certificate of Education was the same thing as the old School Certificate, which it wasn't.

And so there we were when even the army - and when I was a boy, if you were thick you went into the 'army class' - even the army was requiring two A-levels to go to Sandhurst, and the Institute of Chartered Accountants [ICAEW] was requiring 5 O levels to enter into articles. This was the situation. As a result, we recruited in that period of, I don't know, 25 years probably after the end of the war, a mass of people who basically were not in my view fit to be chartered accountants. No doubt an awful lot were, but there were an awful lot who were not.

And you had a great dilution of the quality of the profession. You had this vast explosion in numbers, with industry crying out for accountants. There were chaps - not so much in the big firms, because the big firms maintained their standards - but in the small firms, who would take a boy who had scraped together 5 O levels in a secondary modern school and say: 'Will you come and work for me for nothing?' They were exploited as cheap labour with the bait 'you can become a chartered accountant'. We produced a lot of book-keepers.

Yes. Can I get this in perspective a bit more; you qualified yourself before 1951?

No. I'm one of those who started life as a soldier. I was in the Indian Army. I didn't qualify till 1951. I was in the Indian Army, you see. I came out in 1947 when they gave India away, and had to start to work for my living.

I had family in India; I'd like to go and look at the south.

Next January I go to Pakistan. I'm now chairman of the Great Britain Hockey Board which runs our Olympic hockey side, and we are playing in the Champions Trophy Tournament in Karachi in January. It is a warm-up for the Olympics. And it will be the first time I've set foot in the sub-continent since 1947.

I hope you enjoy many aspects of it.

I shall go from the Alps, where I shall be skiing, and I'll leave my family and beautiful snow to go to Karachi in January!

Can I just finish the point I was developing. Because of this [ICAEW recruitment], there are undoubtedly a lot of practitioners up and down the country who are useless, and there was growing agitation - Eddie [Stamp] started it, going on about the standards of work of the profession. And the reaction of the Institute was, not for the first time in my view, wrong. They said: 'Oh, my goodness: we must lay down standards'. It was a form of hubris on the part of the big firms.

'We will lay down standards because these idiots in the sticks - and 'the sticks' includes people round the corner here, in this city [of London] too - these idiots in the sticks produce an awful product. We have got to show them how to do it, and we have got to lay down firm guidelines, and then, if they stray from those, we can clobber them.'

Now, I believe they could have raised standards anyway. It was not the problem of defining what was bad work. Effectively, like an elephant, you can't define it but you recognise it when you see it. We could still have achieved the aim without this stupid attempt to force people into strait jackets. And this is what has bedevilled the whole thing. They've been so concerned with standards that the basic philosophy of what you're trying to do - how to convey information in a truly meaningful form - has got lost. They want to fit everybody into strait jackets.

But, of course, the funny thing is all the big scandals that occur when accounts go wrong have involved big firms. My own old firm ....

Which was …?

Touche Ross. They were involved in that case where they failed to identify what is cash and what isn't cash. And so this, I think, is where we have lost ourselves. Let me give you two examples. I was hauled up - or I was going to be hauled up - before the Professional Standards Committee a couple of years ago. In a company of which I am a director, the chairman wanted to show certain expenditure, on closing down a subsidiary and moving equipment, below the line. And the auditors said: 'No, we don't think it qualifies as extraordinary expenditure', and there was a bust-up. So they both appealed to me. I'm a non-executive director of this company and I'm an accountant. There is a merchant banker also on the board but he is not qualified.

And, so I looked at the problem. The way this was going to be shown in the accounts, nobody - no share holder - could have been under any misapprehension as to the exact nature of that expenditure; it was clearly spelled out in the form the chairman wanted. So I looked at the Standard. I looked at the various other sets of accounts that the chairmen had produced for similar items in different companies - public companies, of course. And at the end of it, I thought: 'Well, what the hell? Nobody's going to be misled; and if the chairman wants to do it this way, there it is'. I tried to persuade both of them to bend, but they would not. The auditors said: 'We have got to qualify the audit report', and I said: 'Yes, I see you think that you have got a duty to do; you do it'.

Next thing, I get a letter from the Professional Standards Committee saying: 'You're a director of this company; can you please tell us how you voted - whether you voted against the adoption of accounts in this form, and so on'. So I phoned them and explained the circumstances. Then they said, would I like to go and attend. I said: 'No. I've got better things to do'. I picked up the phone and spoke to the Secretary of the Institute - I'm fairly well known in the Institute, as you can imagine. I am not a member of Council or anything, but I'm probably one of the recognised senior members of the body - and that was the end of that. I've never come across such stupidity.

Now I'll give you another example. I am a non-executive director of a quoted company in the building industry. About 10-12 years ago they embarked on property development. The developments were held as stock in trade at the cost of the land and building work, but all interest was written off against trading profits. It eventually got to the state when the auditors said that the completed developments when fully let should be taken out of stock, valued and shown as investment properties. Nobody could quarrel with this.

However, the standard laid it down that the profits on the revaluation of the developments were not brought in as trading profits but the net amounts of them, after tax, were shown below the line and added to reserves. This would have been fine if there had been just one or two developments and no more. But the process continued.

It was not a very large company but a typical year's figures would be: Profit before tax £4.5 millions, Tax £2.25 millions, Distributions £0.75 millions, Retained Profit £1.5 millions. But then there is added below the line net development surplus of £2 millions. The quoted price/earnings ratios were based on £2.25 millions not £4.25 millions. But the treatment adopted conformed with the Standard.

I think this is crazy, because it is misleading shareholders. The basic premise - the basic concept - surely must be to convey information in a meaningful form to the people who can read it. They are not for Aunt Agatha, who from the moment she sees three or four figures joined together runs a mile and says 'I can't understand it' - but for a reasonably informed reader of accounts. I am not saying that it is for an accountant, but for a reasonably informed business man who looking at would say: 'Yes, well that makes sense', and they'll get the message.

Now 70% of the shares are held by institutions anyway.

Yes. But that doesn't mean to say that you can ignore the lay shareholder.

No.

On the other hand when it comes to trust accounts, and I am involved with quite a few, I use a narrative form to convey the information in such a way that it is easily understandable by Aunt Agatha and the other members of the family who have interests. This might be: 'During the year dividends were received as listed on page u totalling £v; tax amounted to £w so that the income after tax was £x; the trustees' expenses were £y, leaving net income of £z. This has been applied as follows'.

This follows what I believe should be the basic premise, that accounts should convey clearly and fairly in a form which can reasonably be acquired by those to whom they are addressed. It seems to me that in its concentration on the nuts and bolts of Standards, the Institute has forgotten this. For example, you will remember the big debate about future tax.

I've just written down 'tax deferral', because I wanted to come onto that.

Under Schedule D, the measure of the income for the year is what the actual income was in the preceding year. The business is deemed to have had that income in the current year for tax purposes, and is the basis of the tax charge for the year. And so there was concern to try and show what the earnings for the year were had the tax charge been based on the actual profits of the year.

The Scottish Institute got counsel's opinion which said it [the tax charge] was a deferred liability, and the English Institute got one that said it was a reserve. On the introduction of Corporation Tax, there was similar concern about showing earnings on a consistent basis, assuming a full tax charge even though it may never be payable. Now consider me as a user of accounts, and particularly as a user of them to value shares.

When you are valuing shares for tax purposes, essentially what you are doing is to put yourself in the position of an imaginary purchaser with an imaginary seller. So, what would actual parties do? I never look at post tax profits - I look at pre tax profits. You must show those on a consistent basis, but the legislature has proved itself amply capable in the last fifteen years of completely changing the whole basis of the tax charge at frequent intervals. Let's go back: we had income tax alone. Then we had income tax plus NDC [National Defence Contribution]. Then we had income tax plus EPT [Excess Profits Tax]. Then we had income tax plus a two-tier profits tax, where you had higher rate on distributions than on retentions, with the rates changing of course all the time. Then you had income tax with a one-tier profits tax. Then you had the Corporation Tax on the classical model. Then you had Corporation Tax on the imputation system.

Not to mention super tax and surtax, in their days.

Yes. In addition to that, you then have stock relief and you have first year capital allowances - all of which means that to try and show a consistent post tax figure is rather like trying to account for changes in the value of money. You are bound to run into nonsense.

What about depreciation; do you add depreciation too, on the same argument?

How do you mean?

If you are looking for profits before tax, there are analysts who add back the depreciation charge, on the grounds that that is also an arbitrary figure.

Well, of course, there is that chap in Manchester who says you do everything on cash flows.

[laugh] Gerry Lawson.

Lawson, yes. No, I don't agree. You see, depreciation is all right. It is an estimate, but then so are lots of other things. If Bacon had written 400 years later, he would probably have written: 'what is profit? quoth jesting Pilate, and would not stay for an answer'.

No, I think you've got to make accounts effective. The only reason you have depreciation is because you are accounting for periods of a year. If you were accounting in periods of 50 years, you wouldn't need depreciation. So, therefore, it seems to me if you are accounting for shorter periods, you have to charge capital expenses against the profits to which they have contributed.

My feeling is that accountants, in the Institute in particular, have been too obsessed with the nuts and bolts - with techniques of doing things - and have lost sight of the object of the exercise. In earlier days, of course, I obviously had to give rather more thought to it than I do now. But I am also looking at accounts daily, from the two points of view - one, of management; and secondly from the point of view of valuing shares.

I'd like to come back to that. But having taken a short detour earlier to ask you when you qualified, can I pick up one or two points?

Yes, do.

You came back to this country and qualified with Touche Ross, did you?

No. I was articled to a firm called Hubbart, Durose and Pain in Nottingham, where it was then the largest firm. It then split up, and it is now very small. It was in its day one of the major provincial firms.

And then you went to Touche Ross after articles?

No. When I qualified, as a matter of simple observation, I had come to the conclusion that partners and managers didn't speak the same language as the finance directors, cost accountants, chief accountants of the companies they were auditing. I always wanted to be in a professional practice, but I went off and I got a job in industry. I had qualified with all sorts of distinctions, and I was fairly well known in Nottingham.

Anyway, I went and became the first chief accountant of a company that was originally called the Hardwick Colliery Company. It was nationalised of course, and on nationalisation, instead of giving the money back to the shareholders as it could have done, they used the proceeds - it wasn't a huge colliery: I doubt if they made more than about £5 or £10 million - to buy a group of family companies. I was the first chief accountant.

Before that, I had an award. In Nottingham, they had - they still have - something called 'Nottingham Roosevelt Memorial Scholarships'. They had a big subscription list when Roosevelt died just before the end of the war, and instead of putting up a statue they used the money to send three young people, mostly men at that time - you had to be under 30 - to the United States every year for three months, just to go and wander around and look at what you were interested in, your particular field of endeavour. They were mostly people in business and the professions. When you came back, the only thing was you had to stand up at a public dinner and tell them what you thought of it for quarter of an hour. And that was it. A marvellous thing. I went on this in 1951.

Just after you qualified.

Yes, within weeks. I had just had my exam results, I think, about a week before I sailed. I went on the 'Queen Mary' and came back on the 'Mauretania'; a very fine trip. The Anglo American Productivity Council had set up a management accounting team.

Just at that time?

No; it was about a year before that. And I knew several people on that. Bill Fea had one of his chaps on it; what is his name? Morrow - Ian Morrow. So I wrote to him; I knew him.

Did he head that team?

I have a feeling he did, yes. So I wrote to Morrow. I already knew a lot of these people because, of course, I was older than the average articled clerk and I was secretary of the student's society.

In Birmingham?

In Nottingham. And unusually I was secretary for two years. As far as I know, nobody before or since had done that. As a result of that, I used to go to a lot of dinners and things round the country, and I always took an interest. We had quite eminent speakers at students' society meetings, and I always used to have to take them out to dinner. And so I got introductions. I went, for example, and had two weeks in the Cadillac Division of General Motors, and they very kindly put me with a very senior chap, a sort of deputy controller and he took me around and showed me all their operations. It was fantastic.

Anyway, after I came back, I did this job for a couple of years. I had said when I took it that I was only going to do it for two years, which they accepted. The group is now Dobson Park, a well known public company. And my successor, as chief accountant, is the present chairman of Dobson Park.

Then, quite by accident, I was at a students' society do. It was a joint debate between two students' societies, and the chairman was Stanley Kitchen. He said his firm were looking for a new partner. They had got two senior partners who had retired or were retiring, and they were looking for somebody to come into the practice. And so I joined them in 1953, and I was there till 1967. I'd had a bad illness in 1966, and the doctors read the Riot Act at me, saying that I was killing myself.

So I left and set up my own share valuation practice. I had no clients, but I knew accountants, solicitors, merchant bankers, etcetera. I did not have a plate up or anything, but, nevertheless professionals from large and small firms have come to me, and it is a very successful practice. I employ one qualified assistant, one secretary, and one chauffeur and I do quite well.

[laugh] Did you get involved in the Birmingham Society?

I was President four years ago.

[laugh] I shouldn't have asked you about it in those terms, then, should I?

Yes. I was on the committee for years, and I was President about 1974/75. I was President of the Students' Society some years before that. Oh yes, I've always been a supporter of the Birmingham District Society.

So your contacts with Bill Fea tended to come through that?

No. I met Bill Fea when I was an articled clerk. He came and lectured to the Students' Society just at the time of that early recommendation on inflation accounting. I was blowing my top to him about it, as you do when you are young. And Bill then very quietly said: 'Well, actually I was chairman of the committee that drafted that' [laugh]. So I duly apologised, and he said: 'No, you go on!' In fact, I still see Bill on skiing holidays; he is a great character. I used to play hockey against him, too.

Well, his company, GKN, were using indexation at this time, weren't they?

Bill was a great fan of a chap called Blackie, at the Caterpillar Corporation in America. You remember, they were pioneers, as was de Paula who had done a lot before the war and who in a way paved the way for the 1948 Companies Act. You had Blackie in America, and to a less extent Bill with Guest Keen and Nettlefold. Frankly, it is my view that the Institute would do far better to encourage its members who are in those sorts of positions - as controllers, chief accountants, finance directors, whatever you'd like to call them - to be venturesome, to try and find better ways of conveying information, and then look at what they're doing and provoke discussion. This way we would get somewhere, rather than having people sitting around tables in Moorgate Place, because no matter what you may do in theory, at the end of the day you need the practical approach. And all the worth-while advances in actual practice have come from the oddball, bright blokes like de Paula who have paved the way. What these [committee] chaps are doing will make sure it [experimentation] will never happen again.

Yes. There is always a compromised version, isn't there?

If you don't comply with the standard, you will get shot. We will tell your auditors to qualify your report. And I tell you, if we had had this approach in the 1930s and de Paula had done what he did with Dunlop's accounts, he'd have had a qualified audit report.

But the debate, even before the standard-setting process was set up, was very much in private, wasn't it? You weren't really getting very much of a public discussion.

I don't know that public discussion necessarily helps. You see when you say public discussion - it is a curious thing. I was always interested in economics; I still am. But, you know, to most accountants economists are highly suspect people: their feet never touch the ground. But, likewise, economists say about accountants: 'Well, of course, their heads never get above the ground!' And they are both right, in a sense. They have been growing together more in recent years, and the more economists have taken an interest in accounting, the more accountants realise there is a bit more to it than 'which side is nearest the window' (i.e. whether an entry is a debit or a credit), so to speak, and the sort of stuff you used to get in basic accounting textbooks.

But nevertheless, accountancy is never going to be more than basic record keeping and reporting. It is just a technique - a sort of technique, an art. But if you haven't got a philosophical base then you've got your head below the ground, and that is what has happened. That is what has happened in the Institute, in my view. There has been far too much tendency to say: 'Bloody economists - we'll show them!'. I think they're making terrible mistakes. I'm too old to take them on now. I am a member of the Association of British Chambers of Commerce [ABCC], and of this place - the Institute of Directors. I'm deputy chairman of the CBI. I advise the Conservative Party on tax policy.

You are a very busy person - clearly so. In fact people such as you who have had some years of experience have got the basis on which to give advice.

In fact, I could never have got on the Council of the Institute because my partner, Stanley Kitchen, was on it.

Well, there are plenty of precedents of having more than one partner in the same firm.

Well, yes - but not in the sticks: not in the provinces. I was in the Birmingham office.

No, I see your point.

It didn't worry me in the least bit. I suppose there was a time when I was a bit younger when it might have been nice, but it just wasn't on, so why bother. I've done a great deal of work for the Institute over the years. I've read papers on the old Summer Courses - I read a paper on estate duty planning.

Did you; when?

1968. I read a paper to the Torquay Conference on the White and Green Papers on capital transfer tax and capital gains tax in 1974. I lectured on some of their tax courses. I enjoy lecturing, and apparently I do it well

Who have been the major tax accountants, going back to Bill Carrington's time? He was clearly the leader during the 1940s.

Talbot - John Talbot.

I don't know him.

John Talbot, of Barton Mayhew; and Lawson - Bill Lawson. They were the ones inside the Institute. The Institute has had a lot of good technologists. I have always taken a much wider view. I am concerned with the philosophy of taxation. I have got a theme I am hammering away at the moment. The big problem at the moment is the higher rates of income tax - the very high marginal rate of tax when National Insurance is added on.

They've got to do something about this. I write memoranda for the Conservative Party now, and the Chancellor too, and for all these bodies making recommendations. I am forever writing papers on tax points. I chaired the CBI Working Party which produced their recommendations on capital taxation, and you will find remarks in there that reflect those of the ABCC and the Institute of Directors and indeed some of the other groups - the Farmers, the Country Landowners' Association - I know the chaps in all these bodies. And you'll find there is a great degree of unanimity of thought.

As an aside on this, what do you think of the rather jaundiced comment recently that accountants have taken over business that solicitors ought to be doing - that the lawyers ought to be doing?

This is the view of the Law Society. Well, of course this is true. And in fact if you look at the origins of the accountancy profession, really they were - they are - effectively a branch of the law, in a sense.

Insolvencies were taken over.

Insolvencies. But lawyers were men of affairs; they used to do this sort of thing. And of course in the tax field, in the States it has developed quite differently. In the States, tax work by and large is the province of the lawyers, and in fact before the tax court only lawyers can be heard. Basically, it is the fault of the lawyers here for letting it go.

When you originally went to Touche Ross in 1953, you were doing general audit there? Or did you immediately specialise in tax at that stage?

No; it was one of those accidental things. In the Birmingham practice, there was a great deal of trust - landed estate - work, and that sort of thing, which I got involved in, and I found it fascinating. And then I got involved in share valuations, and found I was particularly fascinated with this. So although I had responsibility for a certain amount of audit work, I tended to do not so much tax in a sense of the normal tax department - of doing income tax returns and corporation tax computations, which is what they do - but this slightly more esoteric thing: taxation on trusts, and capital taxation, and I got deeply involved in that.

I sat on an Inland Revenue working party some two or three years ago on capital gains in groups of companies. There is still no legislation for them because of the awful business of finding time in the Parliamentary timetable. But when I went on that - I know my capital gains tax pretty well, but company taxation as such was different. I know probably more than the average practitioner, but I don't pretend to be an expert like say Geoffrey Vieler, whom I regard as one of the best people on this subject. Geoffrey Vieler has inherited Bill Lawson's mantle in Binder Hamlyn.

Actually, what was in the back of my mind when I was asking about your specialisation at Touche Ross' was that you were really just too late to be involved with the Millard Tucker report on taxation of income.

Just too late. Oh yes; the fascinating thing about Millard Tucker was, if you read the Minority Report, that it was the basis for the capital gains tax In 1965 - which was pure Nicky Kaldor, of course.

Well, Bill Carrington was arguing very fiercely against any capital gains tax.

People generally came out against it. But it was Nicky Kaldor; the minority report was written by Nicky and it was signed by three people: Nicky, George Woodcock of the TUC and Alan Bullock, who was general secretary of another trades union. But Nicky wrote it. I know. I'm a member of the Addington Society, which you presumably know of?

I don't.

The Addington Society has a closed membership - closed in the sense that it is limited to 60 members. It has got a waiting list. There are ten academics, ten from the bar. The academics ranged from Nicky Kaldor on the left, to [Alan] Prest and others. Harold Edey is a member, although he is not really a tax man.

It was Addington who was the Chancellor who introduced the original Income Tax Act.

The 'temporary tax' that became permanent..!

From the Bar there are people like Charles Potter, and Munro who used to be in practice but is now a Special Commissioner, and most of the leaders from the revenue bar. The ten accountants tend to be, almost without exception, tax partners in the big accounting firms - Price Waterhouse and so on. There are ten tax advisers to big companies, generally ex-Inland Revenue people like Alun Davies of Rio Tinto, Dick Eisan of Shell - people who tend to be ex-Revenue. And there are ten invited members, from the Inland Revenue and so on. We meet four or five times a year at the London School of Economics. We don't usually have to go outside [the group] to get papers. I've read two to them. It is probably the most high powered tax group in the country. Geoffrey Howe is very proud - the thing which he is most proud of in his work since he became Shadow Chancellor is the lecture he gave to the Addington Society two years ago on 'Legislating for Taxation' - you know, this awful problem about how to frame legislation for tax.

Margaret Thatcher came off the front bench in 1974 to understudy Robert Carr, and she led the Opposition in the debates of Standard Committee on the capital transfer tax. She came to the December 1974 meeting of Addington. I'd written this huge paper on Capital Transfer Tax for the Institute, which they had refused to print because they said it was too political. Anyway, she asked me to join a small team advising her on the Bill, and I have been involved with her successors in all the Finance bills since then.

I know the law on share valuations better than anybody outside the Revenue - and better than most people in the Revenue. I was lecturing the other day to the chartered accountants in Stoke on Trent, with a senior chap from the Share Valuation Division. I did one in London here a few months ago, with Harry Booth, who is the Head of the Share Valuation Division, and I can generally shoot them down - particularly on the case law. I know the principles. But it is a combination of that with the fact that I am concerned in the real world with actually buying and selling companies - with advising people, buying and selling shares. I've been involved as chairman of a group in actually being responsible to the outside world for the running of companies in engineering. This gives me quite an advantage.

When I was working in industry, I was mainly involved with engineering, with one or two other companies in the group concerned in other industries. I get a big case, you see, I like to go and visit the factory and walk around and ask questions and get the feel of the thing. Because if I'm going to value a company, it is no good just looking at bits of paper. You've got to get behind them and say: 'Well, what is this thing?'. That is an enormous advantage of mine: I've got a foot in both camps, and to that extent I'm fairly unique.

Yes. The other people I've been talking to have been very much part of the industrial economy, such as Norman Lancaster.

I know Norman well.

He is one of those accountants with a very strong industrial bias. It tends to mean that they are looking for ways to measure income after replacing the fixed assets of the business. They are looking for specific price changes and so on, whereas the practitioners tend to look for solutions you can apply by some form of standard practice.

It is very sad. I think we fall between the two stools, to some extent. For my money, I wouldn't have accounting standards. What I'd do is have a lot more thinking about the name of the game, concentrating on how you convey information in the most meaningful sense. Then I'd leave it to people to do it. As for worrying about bad work, it is much better as I see it to leave it to 'the elephant technique': you can't define it, but you recognise it when you see it. I occasionally see some awful accounts, where practitioners really are doing bad work.

But for tax purposes you've got to have something which is verifiable in some sense, surely, haven't you?

Well, effectively our function, it seems to me, is to convey information to shareholders. Our first duty is not producing something which the Inland Revenue can use.

But there is no doubt that the steam behind the various proposals for inflation accounting comes from the hope that the results are going to be acceptable for tax.

Oh, I'm sure of that. But, in point of fact I am convinced that it is an afterthought, and it wasn't the original reason. In fact, when the Institute came out with current purchasing power, the Sandilands Committee was appointed because the government suddenly woke up to that fact that there is good case law to say that accounts are prepared on generally accepted accounting principles, and the tax must follow the accounts.

They woke up to the realisation: 'My God - these chaps are doing this. They will halve the base upon which we're collecting corporation tax, and we must stop it!' And that was why Sandilands was appointed.

When they started on this road I'm quite convinced that the Institute were not thinking about the tax bills on companies. But people then suddenly realised: 'Of course if we do this, then tax concessions will be the consequence'. But it was not the prior cause of the interest. It may now be.

What do you see as the prime cause?

The prime cause was a fact which was clearly recognisable. If you express accounts in pounds - which is the only thing you can express them in - then the asset that was bought 20 years ago was bought with different pounds from the asset that was bought today. So your yardstick, your measure is no longer a fixed unit. It is stretching all the time - or diminishing, more likely, all the time. And clearly the result is that the conventional accounts can mislead. I mean, you don't mind and I don't mind - we are accountants. You look at accounts and you see there are buildings which you find were bought 20 years ago. You know that they are stated in different pounds.

But the thing that bothers people is that the layman looks at this and says: 'Well, it is a load of rubbish'. In fact, there are those judges who say: 'how can they say those accounts show a true and fair view when they show land and buildings at £100,000 when it is common ground that they are worth a million pounds?'. How can you say that is a true and fair view? That was the rationale in the first place.

I'm quite convinced. Way back - go back to the original work of Bill Fea's committee, and that was what they were concerned about. How can you say that it is a true and fair view? Is it enough for you to say: 'Well, you have to have conventions - and those are the conventions and that is it'? Nobody is saying that is what the assets are worth. All they're saying is that this money in pounds has come into this business from shareholders, either as initially subscribed capital or as profits that they've allowed to be retained in the company. And this is how it has been employed. You've then got this awful problem that they are not in the same pounds - and you've got to try and do something about it.

But, frankly, I do not believe there is going to be - I think it is impossible to find - a perfect solution. Much better therefore, I believe, to allow individuals to go their own way and say: 'Well, this is what we do in our accounts'. ICI, for example, years ago introduced re-valorisation techniques, and they explained what they were doing. All the world saw it, and nobody was misled. And somebody else would have done something else, and so on. And gradually, out of this something would have evolved. But it would have been evolved by practical men trying to solve a practical problem rather than theoreticians. The practising side of the profession looks at it with totally different eyes, as you were saying, and I believe that it is the practical men who would come up with the most practical solution to an insoluble problem. I'm convinced it is an insoluble problem.

Well, there is clearly no perfect solution - no ideal solution.

So let it evolve, rather than try and force it.

You've then got the difficulty that you are going to get a tremendous variety of practice between the progressive firms - the best firms - and the worst ones…

Well, so what?

Presumably the market will have to make some judgement.

When de Paula started producing Dunlop's consolidated accounts, at the same time, there were companies producing accounts in the form they'd been producing them in 1890; it was happening. You could look at published accounts of that era and see the most odd things. People looked at them and made sense of them. Some will convey information in one form, and some will convey it in another. But you're dealing with different businesses, with different problems. I believe you leave it to the company, given the concept that your job is to present the information to the shareholders about their company in a form they can understand. That should be the objective.

So you say: 'Now, you go ahead and have a go at it'. There are certain conventions. You must show certain things; you can't have secret reserves - the Eighth Schedule stuff [8th Schedule of the 1948 Companies Act] - and so on.

But there is no basic reason is there, by the same philosophy, why you should insist on that? If it is not in the interests of the company to show it, why should they be forced to? The shareholders can learn ......

What was that pamphlet that was produced years and years ago, was it by Eaton Place?

By Harold Rose?

Harold Rose: quoting the P&O Steam Ship Company, in 1860 or thereabouts: 'There is some suggestion that we should publish a profit and loss account. Your directors are men of probity in the City. All this would do is to help our competitors!'

Yes.

You've got to go a bit further than that, I think. You've got to say there are certain minimum standards.

But the market can make up its mind who it is prepared to invest in, and who it is not. What I've got in the back of my mind is that there was an article recently from America by Watts and Zimmerman to say that accounting theories are bandied about in a market which is really a market for excuses. And people can pick up a theory that they want if it bolsters their position - and that is fine. And if you look back before we had any direct compulsory disclosure, companies were still disclosing their accounts and people were still discriminating between one company and another on the basis of whether they trusted them.

I don't object personally. I'm frequently accused with being somewhere to the right of Genghis Khan! I'm all for the markets. Every time Margaret Thatcher opens her mouth, she says what I think. And I agree with this entirely. But that doesn't mean to say, I think, that you shouldn't have certain minimum standards of disclosure, if only for this reason alone. That is, you're giving people the privilege of limited liability, and therefore anybody lending money to that company ought to be able to inform themselves sufficiently as to the measure of their risk.

There is no disclosure for partnerships, or proprietorships or unlimited companies. I have an unlimited company for part of our practice. I don't have to publish accounts because anybody who lends money to my company, or anybody who supplies me with goods on credit, knows that he can sue me for it personally.

If the state is going to grant the privilege of limited liability, and it is only the state which can do that, it seems to me that it is entitled to some degree of disclosure. The extent to which you require it is another matter. You may say: 'Well a balance sheet should be enough, because that shows a measure', but I think also a profit and loss account. You could say: 'Well, look at the balance sheet and look at last year's total net assets'. I do not expect you to have to say: 'Well, the profit is the difference between the net worth at the beginning and the end of the year'.

So I think that you've got to have some sort of rules. I think the 1948 [Companies] Act was merely setting out what was best practice - generally accepted practice - at that time. And that is what I think should happen: that legislation should follow best practice, so that if it becomes a general practice of the best people that we show the amount of directors' remuneration, that can be the rule. But don't have it done for political reasons like some of the later stuff, such as political contributions and some of the politically motivated stuff that has come out in recent years. You've got to follow best practices with legislation in this field, not try to lead it. It is not the function of the state to lead it.

Some bright people seem to think that once we get a form of inflation accounting it will be acceptable for tax. I don't think they're going to be able to do this for two reasons - one a theoretical one and one a practical one. I think we may well get something like the Australian system, whereby in effect they do get relief for tax by taking into account the current cost of replacement of stocks. It is a write-off, once and for all. But I find it very difficult to believe that anything beyond something fairly simple like that is going to be acceptable to the Revenue and therefore to the state. Secondly, inflation is not an act of God - it is an omission of government. The Swiss demonstrate this. Any country which has money flowing into it the way Switzerland does ought to have the worst inflation of anybody in the world. Fortunately, the Swiss didn't believe Keynes' theory that politicians and civil servants were the most highly principled people and therefore would never abuse their power

Keynes did also argue that politicians were the prisoners of some long defunct economist ! [laugh].

Keynes is one of the most abused people. It is the neo-Keynesians who basically are the ones to blame for inflation world-wide. The Swiss have never been neo-Keynesian, and they've never had inflation - and in a country which ought to be more prone to inflation than any other single country. But they are sensible: they control their money supply from day one. But there is some hope that at long last the light is dawning here.

The other thing I think is that there is some hope, subject to the hazards of political life, that two or three years from now this won't be a problem any more. It could be that it is a transitional problem. There is nothing that says that inflation is inevitable. Even long before Adam Smith, there have been periods of inflation followed by periods of stability and deflation. So it is only a temporary problem - although temporary may be a long time.

Well, Ricardo seemed to think its something more than that, and Malthus....

Over the long, long period of history, yes - it would appear that there is an inflationary trend, but provided that it is very modest .... Even in the Swiss economy over a very long time there may be some inflation. It probably does not matter much.

Just to ask about this matter of integration, what about the 1957 one first of all [the merger between the ICAEW and the SIAA]? Did you have a view when the Society was talking about integration?

Yes. Of course, the Society - I forget now the statistics - but most of the members of the Society trained in chartered accountants' offices. It was the poor man's way of becoming a qualified accountant, for the chap who couldn't afford articles, and they had a very slightly lower entry standard as I recall. Of course, the chap who had never done his school certificate would have started as the office junior and went on, I think, for quite a long time. And then, if he worked hard at it, he could then enter into whatever they called articles in the Society, and get in by the back door - and a lot of very worthy people got in that way. But by and large the majority of the members of the Society trained in professional offices even if a lot of them went into industry. But I don't think that the proportion in industry and in practice was all that different between the two bodies. As far as I was concerned, I wasn't particularly concerned about it much at the time and was quite happy with that. I had a lot of respect for incorporated accountants. I knew a lot of them, and it was a very similar body to the Institute.

Do you know Eric Davison at Courtaulds?

Eric Davison?

Eric Hay Davison.

Oh yes, slightly - I'm not that familiar with him. And Bertram Nelson of course.

Yes.

A very good man. There wasn't that much difference; it would seem to make sense. But when it came to the integration [of all the CCAB bodies], I was on the committee of the Birmingham District Society at the time. The thing about it that bothered me was first of all that the rationale was wrong - the theory was that all accountants are accountants are accountants and therefore ought belong to one body. And this just isn't true. You've already said something about the difference in attitude of accountants in industry and those in practice.

What really bothered me most was that this would be training in industry. I was blessed if I could see how somebody who did his training in the National Coal Board, or the railways, or the civil service for that matter, how on earth that individual brought up in a totally different environment was ever going to acquire that sort of indefinable thing of being a professional person. Do you remember Angus Maude - Lewis and Maude's book, *Professional People*, where they try to define what is a professional? It is still a very readable book. Angus Maude is my MP, actually; I know him very well. And so that was the first problem.

The second one, and the one that worried me even more, was the argument that was advanced that integration was appropriate since half the membership of the institutes was in industry. There was an assumption that if somebody wasn't in practice or employed in practice, he was in industry, which was rubbish. It was as though the people who'd gone out of it altogether - you would even have the chap who was a clergyman who was classified by the Institute as being in industry, you see. Now, I hadn't got the time, energy or sources of information to be able really to find out how many of the people who were not either in practice or employed in professional offices were in fact even involved in accounting any more. Clearly, a lot of them weren't.

And they said: 'Well, there it is. We have all of these people in industry therefore the sensible thing is to say, 'let's train them in industry'. What concerned me was that, first of all, because of the enormous dilution of the profession in the years since the war, our standards had been allowed to fall, and this was going to reduce them still further. I didn't know in the first place, and nor did anybody else, but it finally emerged at that meeting at the Albert Hall that this invitation had been extended not only to the certified [ACCA] and the cost and works [ACWA] and the municipal treasurers as they used to be called [IMTA], but to all these rag tag and bob tail chaps - the International Accountants, the Faculty of Auditors, the British Accountants: people who were just unqualified, basically. They'd paid over their umpteen guineas to have a certificate to hang on the wall. That strengthened my opposition.

My view was that first of all it would reduce the quality even more. And I didn't say this because I thought that all cost accountants, all certified accountants and municipal treasurers were inferior. As a matter of practical experience, when I was in industry, I had one of the best accountants I've ever met working for me, a man called Smallwood who was a cost and works accountant, a communist Yorkshireman from Hunslet. An awfully nice man: he was an aggressive communist, but he was a brilliant cost accountant - brilliant.

When I went into that job I didn't know 'A from a bull's foot'. I discovered this man was good and I listened to him. And, fortunately for some reason or other, he seemed to respect me and we got on very well and we recruited a number of other first class people. The municipals have always had very high standards - extremely high standards. So in no way was it saying: 'These people are inferior'.

It was basically that, whatever happens to people in the Institute after they have qualified, at least in the first instance they were trained to be practising accountants, with all that that implies. There is some stuff you breathe through the skin, the ethics and the independent attitude of mind. Secondly, if integration had gone ahead, the statistics showed quite clearly that by 1980, of the total membership of this enlarged institute, I think something around 10% was going to be in professional practice, plus perhaps another equivalent number employed in professional offices. All the rest were going to be in industry, commerce, nationalised industries, civil service, local government - you name it.

I took the view - and so did Hugh Nicholson with whom I was associated on this - how can you say this is a body which speaks for practising accountants? How can you go to government, for example, and say you are speaking as this independent body? As I said in one of the debates in the Albert Hall, some snide member of parliament - you can almost hear it in a debate - will say: 'Well, what is this Institute of Chartered Accountants that is making these high and mighty representations? Mr Speaker, I've looked into this and what do I find? 80% of their members are finance directors, cost accountants, chief accountants, city treasurers, this, that and the other. It is nothing more or less than a junior branch of the Institute of Directors!'. I used those words.

And so you had the two basic themes, which were: one, that the Institute was still basically a practising body. We had in fact trained a large surplus and a rather indifferent surplus of members to go off into industry, because it suited some members in practice - it was cheap labour.

It is a way of picking up the right people. You take in large numbers and pick out the one that is good.

Yes, but effectively the chief thing was it was cheap labour. I'm not blaming people; if there is a source of cheap labour, my goodness you use it. But through not raising entry standards, we were recruiting twice as many people as we needed and just allowing them to go through this simple process. I mean, nobody could say the exams in those days were difficult: they weren't. The reason such a small proportion passed even in those days was because the intake was so awful.

Those who did not pass the exams were either really thick, or alternatively had done no work, which was of course the reason in most cases. An awful lot of chaps went in, and, freed from the bounds of school or whatever, they proceeded to think they could do it with a month's cramming at the end. If they went to Caer Rhyn [Hall, a crammer in North Wales run by Ronald Anderson and later by his son], they could; that is all they needed.

In the debates in the Parker Committee, long before integration you remember, on training and so on, I was urging the raising of entry standards. I said then: 'Give me any average intelligent school boy or school girl at 16 or 17, and I will put them in to the final examination at the Institute in six months, and they will pass'. And it was true enough. There was nothing difficult about it.

But still, for all that, we were training people for professional practice. Industry was complaining, saying: 'Chartered accountants are no good'. We weren't training them for industry! And so this argument is then turned round and it is said: 'Industry says we are not training the proper people, so therefore we have got to change our ways and train in industry'. Well, that is losing sight of your objectives. The object of the Institute - the thing it was formed for, and I believe is still the right object - was to provide a professional body for people in public practice. That was the object, and that is what we trained people for. The fact that a lot of people left practice was irrelevant. Just because some barristers have gone off and worked as public secretaries, the Bar doesn't say: 'Well, we ought to train people in company secretaries' offices'.

The Solicitor's Law Society goes some way towards this with these chaps who train in town clerks' offices. I think they're wrong. If that was the underlying philosophy, we were losing our way and secondly you would cease then to be led by practice because inevitably the tail is going to wag the dog. People say: 'Experience shows that the Council will still be run by practising members, because the other chaps haven't got the time'. I say: 'Like hell it will! Somebody like Sutherland will get up and say to hell with this - we will go out and we will recruit support to pull out people on the Council. And you will find your practising members will become a minority'. That was the reason we were against it.

Yes, well in fact that is still feasible isn't it? There is still a majority who is 'not in practice'.

But you see now we have raised the entry standards, and, you know, I feel very sorry for these poor unfortunate kids who have in a sense gone in under false hopes. But when I see the 18% or whatever it is that pass, I am delighted; we are now getting the right people in. I look at these exam papers today and say: 'I would never have passed these'.

What about graduate entry; what is your view on that?

Well, I'm all for it, and I'm on record as having said this - subject, however, to the fact that you've got to have a back door; you must have a back door.

Technician level?

No, I think I would have something rather like the old Society arrangement: somebody who leaves school and for whatever reason doesn't go to university - who may be a late developer, but he takes an interest. All right, let him work for perhaps three years and then say:

'At this point we have a special preliminary exam and if you can pass that exam, you can then enter articles - only we don't call them articles these days. It is ...'

... A training contract.

You can have a training contract, and if you can do it, good luck to you. But, subject to that I would say, yes - graduate entry. It must be. When you have the situation in the educational system that any child of barely average capabilities is pushed to university, or what passes for universities in some cases, what is left has got to be not worth having in general, subject to the odd one here and there. As I say, you allow the back door for that odd one, but not too many.

Yes. I think to some extent that underestimates the extent to which bright children are saying: 'Well, if university is that easy, I don't want to go there'. There has been an appreciable number of school leavers who have actually taken the choice to enter the professions, so they're not interested in university.

Well, if they're bright they'll make it anyway.

Yes, that is right.

If they're bright they'll make it anyway, so you can still have your back door. And after all, if you make it three years which is the length of time you've got to spend at university anyway, there is no time handicap. I think it is a great pity. I entirely agree with the basic premise of the Carr-Saunders report, all those years ago, that effectively the later you start specialisation, the better chance you have of having a more rounded individual.

So you would argue, would you, that there ought to be a fairly basic professional level exam followed by specialisation after the professional exams?

No, I was thinking now about general education. For my money, you see, I've always taken the view that we are not practising a science. Accountancy isn't a science - it is an art, it is a craft. There is no magic to it. It is not an intellectual exercise as, for example, is Greats. If everybody had to do a paper in metaphysics, I would feel a lot happier because it would have really taught them to use their minds and think logically.

Some accounting theory gets extraordinarily close to it! [laugh]

Yes, but to think logically - this is the essence of it. To take a premise and argue logically from that premise, which very few people are capable of doing. And so I don't mind whether the chap has read Greats or read anything else at all; I don't mind. For my money, he is likely at the end of the day probably to be a better accountant than the chap who has done some - I say some - of the accounting courses: you know, 'majoring in accounts', as they say in the States. But you see the States teach much better than we do, or at least they did. I wouldn't know what happens in English universities these days because I don't see them.

The subject has changed a lot in the last decades.

I was very impressed when I was in the States. I had two weeks at Harvard Graduate School - you know, the Business School - on my scholarship tour, and I managed to get myself admitted, believe it or not, but then I couldn't raise the dollars when I came home to send myself there. My father died when I was very young. I hadn't got any money when I came out of the army, but I would have liked to have gone to the Harvard Business School.

You didn't do a university course at all?

I did one year before I went into the army. We read classics.

Good Lord - where?

Nottingham. I was the sole and only under-graduate. This was when it was a university college. I was taking London externals. I was the only student. I had a professor; I had about five, I think, people looking after me. Life was one long tutorial: it was marvellous. But then, of course, I went into the army.

By way of just a bit of a background, my father died when I was very young. My father was in the General Medical Service. My step father, when I left school, said: 'Well, you can be an accountant'. I didn't think much of that. I said: 'Well, I'm not going to sign articles. I want to see what it is like first. You've brought me to the water, but I just want to see and smell the water before I actually drink it'. And so I went off to evening classes, and I swatted like mad on my classics, and I won an exhibition to UCN. It was an enormous amount of money - about £150 a year or so; it was an enormous amount of money in those days.

I was being paid 7/6d a week, prior to signing articles. That is what I would have got 7/6d - a £500 agreement and 7/6d a week pocket money. And there was this - £3 a week. So off I went. I'd have sooner gone to Oxford. In fact there is no doubt in my mind that, if things had worked out differently, I would have certainly been a very highly qualified classicist. Although people would have said it wasn't as good as getting a 1st in Greats, nevertheless I would have been very well educated, I think. But that is a side-track.

I was talking about graduate entry. Yes, I believe it has got to come. And it is happening in effect now, because the school leavers are going to realise that it is only the high flyers that are going to be able to get over this hurdle.

There is a very marked correlation between a high degree class and passing the professional exams.

Well, it is what you would expect after all. I mean, it is nonsense to say 'Examinations are unfair' and all the rest of it. It is absolute rubbish. How else do you test people?

Well, the only grounds for a qualification is whether the examinations really have much intellectual content.

It is coming; they are demanding higher content.

Well, there are some fairly difficult problems.

The basis has got to be technical; it has got to be a question of learning 'which side is the nearest the window'.

If it were purely technical, you wouldn't expect a great advantage to somebody who is intellectually gifted.

Yes, I would. But I wouldn't know; I haven't looked at the exams lately, as to what is in there.

After integration failed, they set up the Morpeth Committee, which was a white-washing exercise. One discovered this later. In fact, on the day of the vote, when the proxies were counted and the result was announced, Nicholson and I went along and attended the meeting at the auditors, the Institute auditors, who were the tellers. And we got 55% against; all we had to get was 33.34% and we were home and dry, and we got 55%. And so Croxton Jones who was the then President invited Nicholson and me to have lunch with him at the Institute. He said that they'd of course known about this for some days and they were going to set up a committee, and they expected that one or other of us should go on it. We looked at each other and said: 'both or none'. So we both went on it.

And it was a completely bogus exercise. Hugh and I took it at its face value. I wrote some long papers for it, and one of the things I said we ought to do was that we ought to have an exam to become admitted as a sort of licentiate member - a sort of probationary member. But if you wanted to practise, then you would after two years have a further exam, and that exam should be a practical exam. In other words, it would be set in such a way that you were asked to write reports; you could have all the text books and everything else to hand, and work as you would work in a professional office.

This wasn't similar to Kenneth Wright's idea that the fellowship should be based on an examination?

No, no, this was quite apart from that. And we said: 'That is how we thought you could go about raising the standards of the people in practice'. If it was felt that you owed some sort of a duty to industry, which we didn't feel, we saw no objection to having anything like the Dip MA, or whatever it was called. But our main concern was to raise the standard of the practising side. I imagine somewhere about there are all the papers I wrote, if you are interested to read them.

Very much so.

But of course it [the committee] was never intended to do more than pick up the pieces. One of the things was the way the Institute was run - we wanted to tackle that. We said it was crazy, and it still is, that a member of the Council has to give something over 400 hours a year of time to the Institute: it was crazy. That is no way to run anything. What we said was a classic example of the wrong way to run it was when they were putting up the new building at Moorgate Place. They had a committee, of course, to do it. Fair enough; of course you have a committee there. But what did they do? The committee has to be members of the Council. There are members of our Institute who are directors of property companies, experts in property, in construction, and all the rest of it. They should have had one or two Council members on the committee and co-opted experts.

I said: 'This is what you should do with all the functional things'. We found, for example, that the Articled Clerks Committee used to meet every month, regularly. All it had to do was to have reported to it the names and numbers and so on of the articles that had been registered in the previous month. And just once in a while where there was some query, they had to make a decision. I mean - members of the Council, from all over the country, to sit in Moorgate Place to do that! Total waste of time!

It wanted one member of the Council to chair that committee, three or four co-opted people - reasonable sorts - to be available, to be consulted in case of need, and that is all it needed. And what a terrible waste of money - bureaucracy gone mad - is spent on running courses. There is a major industry now in the Institute on this. I've been involved in it from when it started, when they first started running technical courses in 1966. They had a pilot course down at Brighton, in May or June 1966. I know because I had this very bad illness - well, I say bad: it was shingles, which doesn't sound bad but I had it all over my head. And my head was literally out here. And the medic said I was very lucky: I was fit, I wasn't over-weight, I was still playing hockey. I've got a very strong heart, but in somebody else it might have been a thrombosis or heart attack. I was lucky it affected me this way. They said, 'whatever you're doing, don't leave your home'.

I was asked to read a paper on the first ever technical course, which was a course for potential lecturers. There were about four or five of us asked to read papers. And I was asked to read a paper: one hour on 'Taxation of gifts and settlements', which of course was crazy. I mean [G.S.A.] Wheatcroft had written a whole book on this subject [laugh]. And I said 'impossible'. So they said: 'Well, that is what we want'. So I said 'right', and I did it. I covered it. And then, of course, I had this illness and I rang up [Michael] Renshall and said: 'What I'll do is I'll have the thing printed off in the office, and if I can't get over this, somebody else will have to read it'. However, I got my chauffeur to drive me down, and I went and I read this paper. I nearly killed myself with the effort. It was the first time I did not enjoy lecturing, and at the end I felt really very weak. Normally, I felt it stimulating. And that was the beginning of courses.

I've been running courses; I used to run them for the Birmingham articled clerks. I started them on their residential courses at Merton College. It was a very good thing. It was one of the earlier ventures of this kind in the country and I've been doing it for years. All this vast bureaucracy at the Institute is a waste of money; they could be run at half the cost. It is not as if the lecturers got paid well; this was one thing that I objected to. Anyway, it all came to nothing. The committee duly reported and practically nothing came of it.

I have gone way over my allotted time with you, and I must impose myself no further. My warmest thanks.

EFERENCES

Allen, D.G. and K. McDermott (1993), *Accounting for Success: A History of Price Waterhouse in America,* Boston, Harvard Press.

Berle, A.A. and G.C. Means (1932), *The Modern Corporation and Private Property*, New York, The Macmillan Company: revised edition (1968), New York, Harcourt, Brace and World.

Bonbright, J.C. and G.C. Means (1932), *The Holding Company,* New York, McGraw Hill.

British Accounting Review - Special Edition, June 1997.

Chandler, A.D. (1977), *The Visible Hand: The Managerial Revolution in American Business*, London, Belknap Press.

Chandler, A.D. (1990), *Scale and Scope: The Dynamics of Industrial Capitalism*, London, Belknap Press.

Mann Judd Gordon & Company (1967), *Interim Account of a Going Concern: Some Essays on the History of the Firm of Mann Judd Gordon & Company, Chartered Accountants Glasgow, circa 1817 to 1967, on the Occasion of the 150th Anniversary of its Foundation,* Glasgow.

May, O. (1943), *Financial Accounting New York*, Macmillan reprinted Lawrence [Kansas] Scholars Book Co. (1973) p.9.

Mumford, M. (1979), 'The End of a Familiar Inflation Accounting Cycle', *Accounting and Business Research,* pp. 98-104.

Mumford, M. (1983), 'Accounting for Inflation: a review article', *Accounting and Business Research*, pp. 71-82.

Noguchi, M. and J. Edwards (2004), 'Accounting Principles, Internal Conflict and the State: The Case of the ICAEW 1948-1966', *Abacus,* Vol 30, No.3, pp.280-320.

Norris, H. (1947), *Accounting Theory: an outline of its structure*, London, Pitman.

Shackleton, K. and S.P. Walker (1998), *Professional Reconstruction: the co-ordination of the accountancy bodies 1930-1957*, Edinburgh, ICAS.

Shackleton, K. and S.P. Walker (2001), *A Future for the Accountancy Profession: the Quest for Closure and Integration 1957-1970*, Edinburgh, ICAS.

Smallpeice, B. (1981), *Of Comets and Queens*, Shrewsbury, Airlife Publishing Co.

Stacey, N.A.H. (1951), *English Accountancy*, London, Gee & Co.

Stamp, E. and C. Marley (1970), *Accounting Principles and the City Code*, London, Butterworths.

Sweeney, H.W. (1936), *Stabilized Accounting*, New York, Harper.

Walker, R.G. (1978), *Consolidated Statements*, New York, Arno Press.

Walker, S.P. (ed) (2005), *Giving an Account: Life Histories of Four CAs*, Edinburgh, ICAS.